Dictionary of Bowing and Pizzicato Terms

4th Edition

Joel Berman
Barbara G. Jackson
Kenneth Sarch

TABLE OF CONTENTS

ACKNOWLEDGMENTS

Appreciation is extended to the three co-authors — Joel Berman, Barbara Jackson and Kenneth Sarch, for the many hours they committed to the realization of this dictionary in its revised and expanded form. Further kudos go to Kenneth Sarch for his responsibilities of coordinating the authors' efforts as well as for his proofreading expertise. Please consult the bios found on page 69.

Special thanks are extended to violinist Jack Glick for his suggestions and comments concerning the twentieth century pizzicato terms in the dictionary, and to Sonya Monosoff for her helpful suggestions.

Appreciation is extended to Anne Sheldon for her assistance in proofing/editing final copy.

Melissa Becker, a graduate student at The Pennsylvania State University School of Music, was especially helpful in researching and gathering musical examples.

A special word of thanks and appreciation goes to Genley Anderson of Williamsport, Pennsylvania, whose skill with the computer, photographic processes and string repair knowledge were invaluable to the project. Mr. Anderson spent a great deal of time retyping text, redesigning format, editing text, adding photos and reconstructing musical examples. The cover of the publication includes a photo of three bows provided by Mr. Anderson. In addition, he provides an insightful statement about bows based on his own extensive experience.

Robert L. Cowden
ASTA

PREFACE

We are pleased to present this revised and improved Fourth Edition of the **Dictionary of Bowing and Pizzicato Terms**. As wonderful and useful as the Third Edition proved to be, we discovered a number of items that needed to be changed, enhanced, streamlined, clarified and occasionally omitted in order to make the dictionary even more useful and attractive.

The more noticeable things were:

- integrating twentieth century terms from the back of the previous edition into the main dictionary entries
- changing the entries from all capital to upper and lower case **bold** letters
- making the musical examples consistent in format with titles above and descriptions below
- adding photo illustrations and an attractive cover

Each of the authors worked through every definition to edit, clarify, refine and rewrite. The new edition reads and looks much better than its predecessor.

The bowing terms contained in this volume serve to name the various ways in which string players use the bow to draw wonderful and magical sound from string instruments. Every nuance of tone we produce on a string instrument comes to life at the command and coaxing of the bow. The bow is the string player's paintbrush, the breath which gives life to our song, the sword with which to battle the virtuosic challenges of pyrotechnical passages, the whip to drive the horses, and the pen which brings forth the poetry.

Pizzicato techniques and terminology in the twentieth century have been expanded to include many new, imaginative and virtuosic elements. It used to be that you either plucked the string or you bowed it. Today there are a myriad of new pizzicato possibilities. Pizzicato is played in many different locations to obtain various tone colors. Snap, nail, strumming, chords and other pizzicato methods are a part of what string players do. From Paganini through the twentieth century the string player has had to develop plucking techniques worthy of a guitarist. It is surprising that, in this last decade of the twentieth century, many string players still play and composers still ask for pizzicato in the same traditional, unimaginative way. The need to list and describe the many new pizzicato innovations used in twentieth century music encouraged us to include this extra section in this edition of the dictionary.

Kenneth L. Sarch
Project Coordinator

FROM WHENCE COMETH THE BOW?

If we can say that the violin is an Italian invention (in a most general sense), then we can say that the bow, as we know it today, is a French invention. The reason for French pre-eminence in this field is the result of a charming bit of serendipity that has nothing to do with instruments or music.

In the 17th and 18th centuries, Paris was one of the most important textile design and production centers in the world, and a wide variety of organic dye stuffs were imported by this industry. Many of these, including madder for red, black, purple and brown; woad and indigo for the blues; saffron and turmeric for the yellows, had been in use for a very long time in the textile and printing industries. As commerce increased with the Americas, especially in the late 17th century, the dyewood Pernambuco (Ceasalpinia echinata) began to be imported in vast quantities from Brazil to be processed by the dye industry to produce a brilliant purple-red color. Thus, Pernambuco became the wood of choice for the early French bowmakers (i.e., prior to F. Tourte) and subsequently became the wood from which fine bows were made. The wood that is commonly known as "Brazilwood" is really the same species, coming from the sapwood of the tree while "Pernambuco" derives from the heartwood.

The wide availability of the raw material for violin bows was a tremendous advantage for these bowmakers since they could afford the luxury of exercising very high standards with regard to the inherent qualities of the wood itself. Any samples that did not meet their criteria could easily be re-sold to the dyewood supplier. It is for this reason, *in general terms*, that we tend to find the highest quality Pernambuco in French bows from the late 17th century up to the early 20th century.

An interesting activity that I use in lecturing, especially with young people, is to take a quantity of Pernambuco shavings and make a simple solution with plain water. Almost immediately a strong infusion of the characteristic purple-red color results.

An area that is of great interest to the player involves determining what is a "good" bow. A fair amount of work has been done in attempting to objectively quantify the characteristics of bows, but these efforts, in my opinion, fail to recognize the fact that subtle differences in the measurements of the bow stick reflect variations in the material itself. Recall that the bow is, like the violin, a complex object made of wood, and since the qualities of the wood are so variable, it is incorrect to try to adhere to a set of constant values for the dimensions of the bow. A metaphor that I'm fond of is that bows are like shoes -- what feels comfortable to one person may be quite uncomfortable to another even though both people wear the same size. I once had the experience of being with the concertmaster of a well-known orchestra who had played Itzhak Perlman's violin and bow and found that he could not make Perlman's bow bounce. I heard the concert with Perlman playing some Paganini during an encore, and I can unequivocally state that the bow did bounce quite well!

I also need to emphasize that price is not always a reliable indicator of playing qualities. An inexpensive stick may have playing characteristics that equal or even surpass more expensive sticks. The price of a bow reflects the reputation and antique value of the maker, how the bow is mounted (silver or gold versus nickel), and the maker's and seller's estimate of the market value of the bow. An example that comes to mind is an anecdote from my shop where a famous concert violinist preferred a cheap Brazilwood bow with commercial nickel mounts to other bows in his collection, including bows by Peccatte, Voirin and a gold, diamond and ruby mounted Kittel!

The best advice I can give to a string player is to gain as much experience as possible in playing with a wide variety of bows, and realize that the requirements for playing music in one style may be at odds with those for another. Also, over time, one's technique and control may change and the qualities of a favorite bow may later be found lacking.

Genley Anderson

Bibliography:

Les Archêts Francais
Author: Ettien Vatelot
Publisher: M. Dufour, 9 Rue Rogemont á Paris

A History of Printed Textiles
Author: Stuart Robinson
Publisher: M.I.T. Press, Cambridge, MA

STANDARD BOWING TERMS

abgesetzt, abgesetzet, (G.) Separated; often used together with
or as a synonym for abgestossen, the usual German term for *staccato* (in
the generic sense of the term, not the particular type of bowing).
Historically, Quantz uses *abgesetzet* to mean lifting the bow from the
string and replacing it. He states that the bow is lifted and replaced on
the string in such passages as:

1) in syncopated rhythms, in which the bow is lifted after the syncopated note to give a lively expression to the rhythm

2) after the note preceding an appoggiatura, for greater clarity;
3) in rhythmic patterns in which two down-bows are used in succession, such as

or

and

4) in passages marked with dashes (*Strichelchen*) or labeled *staccato*, as long as the notes are not too fast. Eighth notes in *allegro* movements and sixteenth notes in *allegretto* tempo are considered too fast for lifted bows; Quantz says that the bow
   should not leave the string when playing them, as they will

sound hacked or whipped. Separation (*Absatz*) is used in the pattern

in *allegro*, with successive up-bows as indicated, but the bow is *not* lifted. A succession of lifted up-and-down-bows may be found only in passages of moderate speed. (Quantz, *Versuch einer Anweisung die Flute traversière zu spielen*, 1752). By 1802 when Koch's dictionary was published, *abgesetzet* was simply a synonym for *abgestossen*. (Koch, *Musikalisches Lexikon*, 1802). The term is used by other writers to indicate merely a separation between notes, without any implications of the degree or means of separation.

See *abgestossen, détaché, piqué, reprise d'archet, spiccato, staccato, and stoccato.*

abgezucht (G.) An eighteenth century term listed by Walther as a synonym for *détaché*. (Walther, *Musikalisches Lexikon*, 1732). Obsolete.

above fingers (abbreviated AF). A 20th century term used for cello and bass to indicate a special bow placement on the string between the left hand fingers and the nut. This produces a tiny, distant and muted tonal effect.

absetzen (G.) To play with separated bow-strokes. See *abgesetzt*.

abgestossen (G.) *Staccato* (in the generic musical sense); the normal term in German for musical *staccato*. Gestossen is also occasionally used in this sense. (Mozart, *Gründliche Violinschule*, 1756). The non-musical meaning of the root of these terms in fencing is similar to that of the Italian term *stoccata: stossen*, to thrust, stab, or strike; *stoccata*, a rapier-thrust. Thus the implication, when these terms were first used as technical terms in music, may have been a vigorous type of separation. In time, the meaning came to mean *staccato*, without specifying the means of separation. See *détaché, gestossen, staccato, stoccato*, and *stabb*.

abstossen (G.) To play staccato. See *abgestossen, détaché, staccato*.

Abstrich (G.) See *down-bow*.

alzare l'arco (It.) To lift the bow.

Anstrich (G.) See *up-bow*.

arcata, arcato, archata (plural = arcate) (It.) Bow or bowed. See *arco*.

> ___ *in su.* See *up-bow*.
> ___ *in giú.* See *down-bow*.
> ___ *con larga.* With full bow-stroke.
> ___ *grande.* Full-bow-strokes.

Historically:

1) A note or group of notes with one bow, or a long note with one bow. (Cerreto, *Della prattica musica*, 1601; Rognoni, *Selva de varii passaggi secondo l'uso moderno*, 1620).

2) A long expressive note on one bow, with crescendo and diminuendo, and with vibrato. "Nothing of their [Italian] playing is so difficult as the arcata or long bow, with which they will begin a long note, clear, without rub, and draw it forth swelling louder and louder, and at the acme take a slow waver; not trill to break the sound or mix two notes, but as if a bird sat at the end of a spring, and as she sang the spring waved her up and down, or as if the wind that brought the sound shaked, or a small bell were struck and the sound continuing waved..." (North, "The Art of Gracing", c. 1700, in Wilson (ed.) *Roger North On Music*, 1959). This expressive meaning may be a misunderstanding of the Italian term by the English; North is the sole source for such an elaborate definition of the term.

3) *Arcata* is used to mean simply *bowed*. It is frequently part of a phrase describing various bowing or musical effects:

    > ___ *morendo.* Expressive bow stroke with diminuendo. (Monteverdi, *Il combatimento di Tancredi e Clorinda*, 1624).
    > ___ *solo forte piano.* Forte and piano in one bow-stroke. (Ibid.)
    > ___ *sciolte.* Free bowing, that is, not bound by slurs; may be articulated in a light detached bowing of some sort. (Walther, Scherzi, 1676).
    > ___ *sostenute e come sta.* Sustained bows without ornamentation. (Corelli, Op. 6, no. 8, "Christmas Concerto"). This

designation is necessary to prevent the performer from improvising ornamentation on long notes. It only occurs once in Corelli's works.

Violin Concertato I

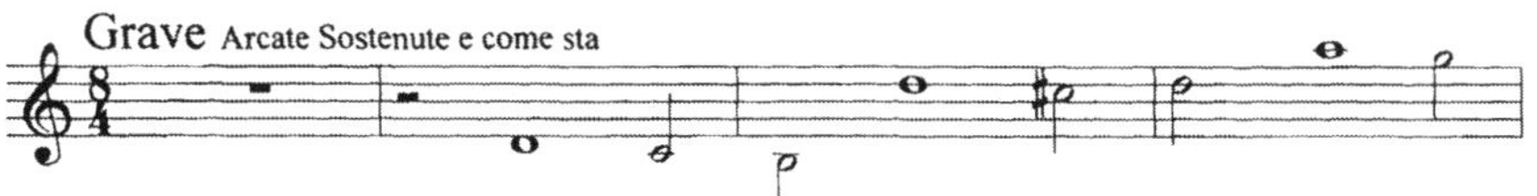

    __ *lunghe.* Long bow-strokes with smooth connections. Pincherle (*Vivaldi*) suggests that it also means "without ornamentation" and is synonymous with the more common indication *come sta* (as it stands). It is Vivaldi's equivalent of Corelli's term above.

    __ *arcate* (pl.) *mute.* Changing bow strokes. "The violin calls for beautiful passages (*passaggi*), distinct and long, with playful figures and little echoes and imitations repeated in many places, impassioned accents, changing bow strokes (*arcate mute*)...." (Agazzari, *Del sonare sopra il basso*, 1607).

archet (F.) Bow.

    au milieu de l' __ In the middle of the bow.

    avec le dos de l' __ See *col legno.*

    avec toute la longueur de l' __ With the whole-bow.

    bout d' __ Bow-tip.

    coup d' __ Bow-stroke.

    du bout de l' __ At the bow-tip.

    en jetant l' __ "Thrown bow." See *jeté, spiccato, ricochet.*

    frappé avec l' __ Strike the string with the bow-stick. See *legno* (Techniques No.2), *battu, battuto.*

    glisser tout le long de l' __ Whole-bow.

    l' __ bien à la corde. Very legato.

    l' __ de toute sa longueur. With whole-bow.

    lever l' __ Lift the bow.

    moitié de l' __ Half-bow.

    moitié inférieure de l' __ Lower half.

    moitié supériore de l' __ Upper half.

    tout l' __ *sur chaque note.* With whole-bow on each note.

4

arco, archetto (It.) Bow or bowed.

a metá l' __ With half-bow.

alzare l' __ To lift the bow.

__ *magno* Probably means *grand détaché*. (Tartini, *L'art du violon*, 1798).

__ *per* __ Separate bow- strokes; non-slurred.

battuto coll __ See *legno* (Techniques No. 2), *battuto*.

col __ *naturale* Bow in a normal manner (following a passage played *sul ponticello, sul tasto* or other bowing). See *modo ordinario, ordinario, ponticello, tasto*.

colpo d' __ Bow stroke.

con l' __ *in tutta la sua lunghezza*. With the whole bow. See *whole bow gliding*.

con molto __ With much bow.

gettando l' __ See *jeté*.

gran __ Whole-bow. See *grand détaché*.

lasciate ondeggiare l' __ Let the bow undulate. See *ondeggiando*.

metà inferiore dell' __ Lower half.

metà superiore dell' __ Upper half.

tutto l' __ Whole-bow.

punta d' __ At the point (tip) of the bow.

arpège, arpègement, harpège (F.) See *arpeggio*.

arpeggio, arpeggiando, harpegiato, (It.), *arpège, arpègement* (F.) Notes of a chord played in rapid succession, particularly, in string playing, a chord on three or four strings. In the following passage, the *legato* style arpeggiation evolves into a springing *ricochet*.

Mendelssohn, *Violin Concerto in E Minor*, Op. 64
(1st movement cadenza)

Example of *arpeggiation*

Springing arpeggio is a slurred arpeggio in which the bow is allowed to jump or spring, as in the last groups of the above example. This bowing is indicated by the combination of dots and slurs shown. See *legato, ricochet*.

Historically:

1) "Manner of playing the different notes of a chord successively and rapidly instead of striking them all at one time. There are instruments on which one cannot form a full chord except by arpeggiation; such instruments are the violin, violoncello, the viol and all those which one plays with the bow, because the convexity of the bridge prevents the bow from pressing against all the strings at once. For making chords on these instruments, one is obliged to arpeggiate, and as one can only draw forth as many sounds as there are strings, the *arpeggio* of the violoncello or of the violin will not consist of more than four tones. It is necessary for the arpeggio that the fingers be arranged on the strings and that the arpeggio be drawn by a single large bow-stroke which begins strongly on the largest string and comes to an end shaping and diminishing the sound on the top string... That which is done on the violin out of necessity, one practices for reasons of taste on the clavecin." (Rousseau, *Dictionnaire de musique*, 1768). This is a typical, though unusually carefully worded, description of the method of playing all chords of three or four notes in seventeenth and eighteenth century string music.

2) *Arpeggio* is also used to indicate that a succession of chords is to be played in broken patterns. The term is often written in the music and indicates that the performer is to improvise the arpeggiation pattern for the written chord progression. A wide variety of such patterns, using slurs, separate bow strokes, or both, is given in the instruction books of the time as examples for the student. Details of the method of arpeggiation may or may not be prescribed by the composer, the pattern may be completely written out, or described in more general terms, or left completely to the performer's discretion. A typical list of types of *arpeggio* patterns follows:

Vivaldi, *Violin Concerto* Op. 3, No. 10

Ex. 1

6

Ex. 2 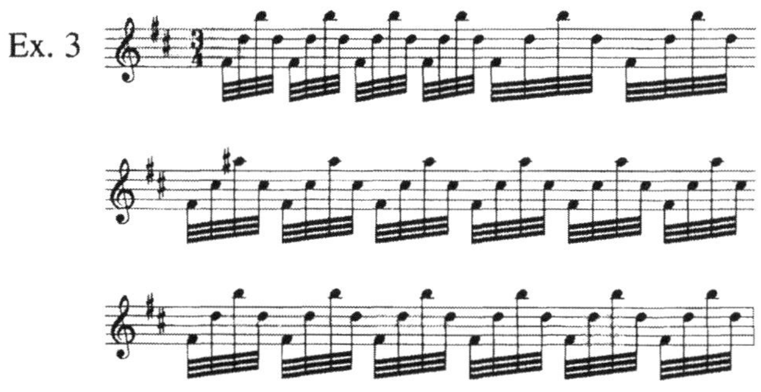

Ex. 3 

Ex. 4

Walther, *Hortulus Chelicus*, 1688

Ex. 5

Ex. 6

arpeggio sempre legato (It.) *Arpeggio* always slurred (Ex. 1 & 2)
arpeggio leggato [sic] (It.) Slurred *arpeggio* (Castrucci, 1730)
arpège aller et retour (Fr.) *Arpeggi* in both directions (Duval, 1715)
arpeggio battuto di biscrome (It.) *Arpeggio* in thirty-second notes.
    (Ex. 3)
arpeggio sempre sciolto, arpeggiando con arcate sciolte (It.)
    Arpeggi detached throughout (Ex. 4 & 5)
arpeggio-ondeggiando (It.) Slurred oscillation between two notes
    on adjoining strings

For a term of doubtful meaning which might possibly be connected with a form of arpeggio, see *ricochet* (historical meaning). Other spellings include *harpége* (F.), *harpegiato* (It.), *harpeggio* (It.), *harpeggiato* (It.).

articulation (E.) In modern usage, a general musical term referring to the means of giving clear definition and shape to individual notes or to phrases. In string playing the means of articulation include techniques of both the right and left hand. For the bow, the term refers to methods of phrasing, stopping, lifting and attacking with the bow.

Historically:

French composers used notes marked with dots, apparently to be played with a light, off-the-string bowing, usually eighth notes. (Mondonville, *Les sons harmoniques*, c. 1738) This term may also be used in the general sense of somewhat separated notes, without indicating the degree or means of separation.

articulé, coup d'archet (F.)

Historically:

1) "When the notes of a run (*roulade*) are slurred (*liées*) all together, or two by two, or three by three, etc., and when there is a dot over each of the notes, this ... designates the coup d'archet articulé; the wrist ought to be very free for making this bow-stroke well, and ought to articulate unaided each of the notes with a perfect equality, whether they are those on the up-bow or those on the down-bow." (L'Abbé le fils. *Principes du violon*, 1761).

Example of *coup d'archet articulé*

This stroke is similar to the modern up-bow or down-bow *staccato*. It is widely used in the music of Italian virtuosi of the eighteenth century such as Locatelli and Veracini, and that of French masters like LeClair. Among the earliest references to this stroke are those of Marais (*Pièces de viole*, 1701) and Piani op. 1, 1712). Piani describes the stroke as "equal notes, articulated by a single bow stroke." The emphasis on equal notes is not merely an admonition to use skill and care to make the stroke even but is also a warning that the *note inégale* (unequal note, a rhythmic device common in French music of the time) is not to be used with the *coup d'archet articulé*. Though the term is French, the origin of the stroke is Italian. It is also found in the Biber Sonatas (17th cent.) and in Walther, *Hortulus Chelicus* (1698).

2) Several notes may be detached in one bow-stroke by *lifting* the bow for each note. The number of notes may be two or may be as high as a dozen. In the French edition of Mozart's *Violinschule, articuler* is the term used for this manner of bowing. No differentiation in the marking for a lifted or on-the-string series of notes on a single bow-stroke is found in most of the music of the period, although Quantz (*Versuch*, 1752) uses dots under a slur for articulated notes on one bow which remain on the string and vertical dashes for a series of lifted notes. In most music of the eighteenth century, however, the player must decide for himself which type of bowing is appropriate. See *craquer l'archet, Erhebung des Bogens.*

attacca alla corda (*con l'arco attaccato alla corda*) (It.) "Fasten to the string" or "with the bow attached to the string." These phrases are used by Vivaldi to indicate a *smooth*, connected style of playing. In the Concerto PV 419, in which another part is marked with vertical dashes, the attaccato indication may imply that the bow is on the string in contrast to the notes with the dashes; thus the vertical dashes may be an indication for off-the-string bowing.

aufgehoben (G.) The term used by Leopold Mozart (*Gründliche Violinschule*, 1756) to describe the lifted bow. The term may still be found in some German sources.

Aufstrich (G.) See *up-bow*.

balzato (It.) Bouncing.

bariolage (F.) A passage which idiomatically exploits the distinct, individual *timbres* of the various strings. In this bowing style, no two consecutive notes of a passage of disjunct figuration are played on the same string. Instead, the bow oscillates between two, three, or four strings. Occasionally, a passage employing the *bariolage* principle will require the reiteration of notes.

J. S. Bach, *Partita in E Major*

Example of non-slurred *bariolage*

Brahms, *Symphony No. 4 in E Minor*

Example of slurred *bariolage*

Historically:

"A collection of different colors mixed without rules." (Furetière, *Dictionnaire universelle*, 1701) This term is not found in any theoretical or didactic works dealing with violin-playing until after the middle of the eighteenth century. In the early nineteenth century it is finally fully defined with three meanings as a technical term in music:

1) a passage in which notes are played on different strings for reasons of contrasting colors of sound,
2) a passage in which stopped notes on one string alternate with an adjacent open string, and
3) a passage using open strings where normally stopped notes would be used.

Though the term bariolage is found in theoretical sources only after the mid-eighteenth century, the technique is found in violin music of various styles from the time of Corelli on, with either detached or slurred bowings. See *ondeggiando*.

batterie (F.) *Eighteenth Century*: "Manner of striking and repeating successively on different strings of an instrument the different sounds which make up a chord, and of moving thus from chord to chord by a like movement of notes. *La batterie* is only a continuous arpeggio, but one in which all the notes are detached instead of being slurred as in the arpeggio." (Rousseau, *Dictionnaire de musique*, 1768) Sets of examples of patterns for *la batterie* are commonly found in violin method books.

Three examples from Corrette's
L'art de se Perfectionner Dans le Violon, 1782, follow:

Ex. 1

Ex. 2

Ex. 3

Examples of *batterie*

battu (F.) Hit or tapped (with the bow stick). See *legno* (Techniques No. 2), *archet, frappé avec l'.*

battuto, battuto coll'arco (It.) Strike or tap the string with the bow stick. See *legno* (Techniques No. 2).

behind the bridge (E.) *Twentieth Century*: Producing high-pitched indefinite tones by bowing or plucking on the strings between the bridge and the tailpiece. Clear, high-pitched tones are obtained with a bow placement either close to the bridge or close to the tailpiece (on the string wrapping). Bow placement in the middle produces a scratchy, unpitched noise. The notation for *behind the bridge* is not standardized; each composer uses a different symbol for this effect.

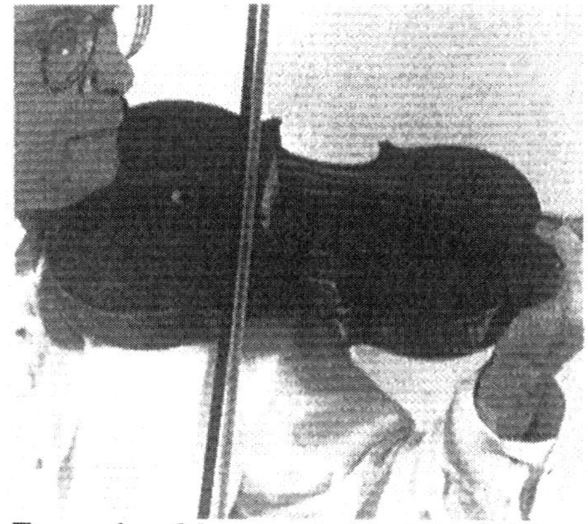

Example of *bowing behind the bridge.*

behind left hand fingers (E.) *Twentieth Century*: An instruction for a string instrument to indicate that the bow is placed on the string near the nut at the beginning of the fingerboard (in first position) on the "wrong" side of the left hand. The tone color thus produced is quite haunting and soft, small and distant. The composer's notation needs to show both where to finger as if the notes are to be sounded normally and the actual pitches produced with the bow in back of the left hand. The pitches come out in reverse from normal bowing: Low fingers produce high pitches; high fingers produce lower pitches. 1,2,3 sounds high-lower-lower and the lower fingers cannot be held down but must be lifted to produce the next pitch. Also, it is not practical to play *behind the left hand fingers* on the *middle two strings* as they are too close together. An unfortunate side effect is the rosin left on the string in first position-this must be cleaned off to avoid sticky fingers for the violin and viola. Two techniques make this effect easier to negotiate:

Example of *behind left hand fingers.*

1) Take the left hand off the fingerboard and reverse it so that the thumb and first finger are now closer to the performer than the fourth finger. Fingering in this reversed position (fingers now on the G string side of the neck) allows normal fingering (low finger = low pitch) and anchoring the hand.

2) When sitting, hold the violin or viola vertically (like a viol or cello) on the lap. Although this makes bowing near the nut more comfortable, it does not allow for technique no.1, reversing the left hand. See *above fingers.*

Bindung (G.) Slur.

Bogen (G.) Bow.

   __ mitte. Middle of the bow.

   ganzer __ Whole-bow.

   in der Mitte des Bogens. In the middle of the bow.

   langer __ Long bow-stroke.

   mit aufgeworfenem __ Literally, "thrown bow." See *jeté, spiccato, ricochet.*

   mit der ganzen Länge des __ Whole-bows. See *whole bow gliding.*

   mit liegendem __ On the string, smoothly.

   springender __ Bouncing bow-strokes. See *spiccato, sautillé.*

   mit dem __ geschlagen Strike the string with the bow.

   mit springendem __ Bouncing bow-strokes. See *spiccato, sautillé.*

   viel __ Full bows.

Bogenführing (G.) Bowing.

Bogenwechsel (G.) Bow change.

   viel __ Many bow changes (on a long sustained tone).

   kein __ No bow change.

bois (F.) Wood (bow stick). See *legno.*

   avec le __ With the wood.

   sur le __ On the wood.

bombi (It.) Seventeenth and eighteenth century term for *tremolo.* (Printz, *Musica modulatoria vocalis*, 1678). See *tremolo.*

bow (E.), *archet* (Fr.), *archetto* (It.), *arco* (It., Sp.), *Bogen* (G.)

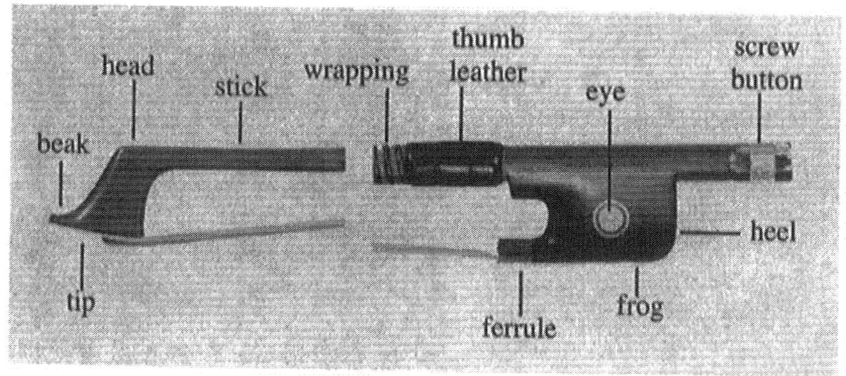

Parts of the Bow

13

bowing (E.) The art of producing sound from a string instrument using the bow.

Twentieth Century Terms:

___ *under the strings* (E.) An unusual and rare bowing procedure in which the string player turns the bow completely over and presses the bow hair against the string *underneath* the usual playing area (between the bridge and the fingerboard). Of course, underneath the strings the curve is inverted so that only the outer two strings (highest and lowest) can be played (see illustration). When the outer strings are fingered in various combinations, widely spaced double stops can be obtained by this upside down bowing method. For example, a two octave double stop! However, because of limited space to play underneath the strings and the awkwardness of this device, only simple and isolated musical effects are possible.

Example of *bowing under the strings*

___ *behind the bridge* (E.) See *behind the bridge*

___ *on the side of the bridge* (E.) A special buzzing sound created by drawing the bow hair with pressure against the side of the bridge thus causing the bridge to vibrate. This buzzing tone is higher on the violin and viola and lower (a kind of rumbling sound) on the cello and bass.

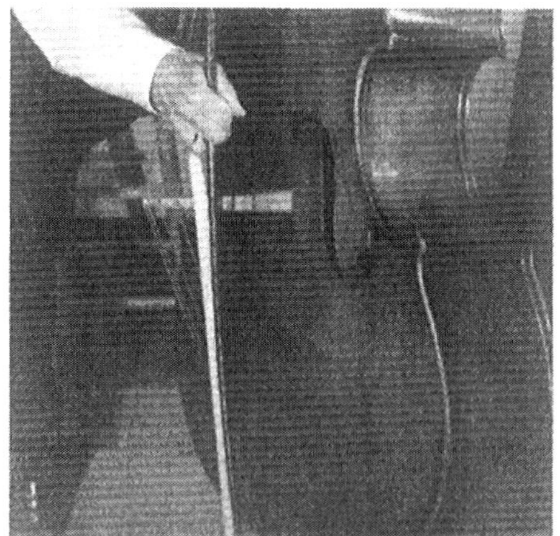

Example of *bowing on the side of the bridge*

__ *on the endpin spike* (of cello and bass) (E.) A low rumbling sound can be produced by pressing the bow hair against the endpin spike and vibrating the spike by drawing the bow across it.

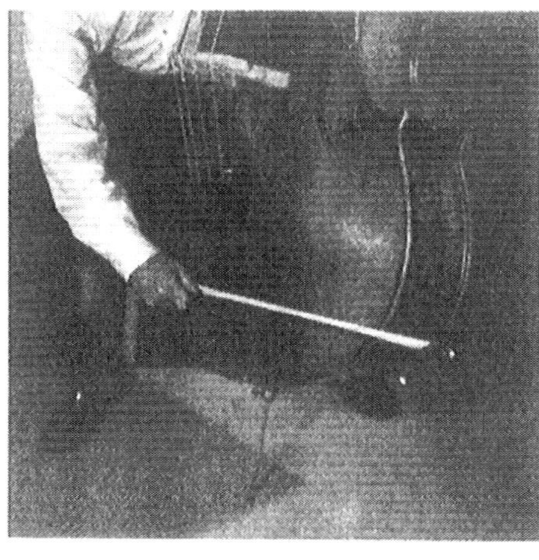

Example of *bowing on the tailpiece*

__ *on the tailpiece* (E.) Another type of buzzing sound created by drawing the bow across the tailpiece with sufficient pressure. Again, the buzzing is lower on the cello and bass.

__ *on the tailpiece hanger* (E.) Vibrating the nylon or gut hanger that attaches the tailpiece to the endbutton by drawing the bow slowly across it producing a shrill and penetrating tone.

__ *on the strings in the peg box* (E.) Placing the bow upon the strings inside the peg box and drawing the bow across them producing a soft, high-pitched squeal.

brechen (G.) To break (a chord). "If a chord, or other musical pattern, is articulated (*tractirt*) and set in motion (*gerührt*) not all at once but one note after the other." (Walther, *Musikalisches Lexikon*, 1732) See *arpeggio*.

breit gezogen (G.) Broadly drawn; with whole bows.

breit gestrichen (G.) Broadly bowed.

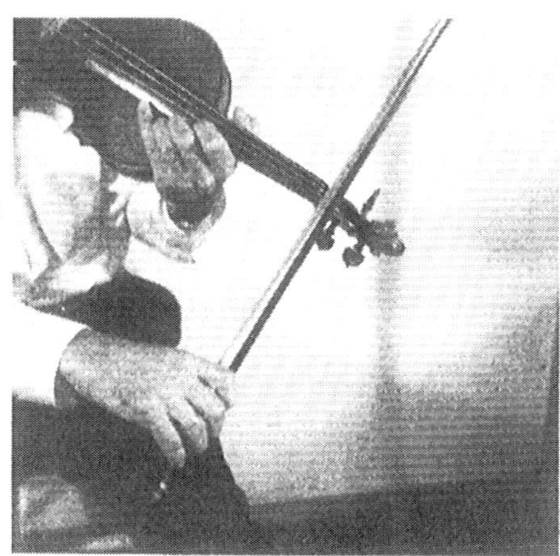

Example of *bowing on the strings in the pegbox*

brisure (F.) Passages involving two strings which are not adjacent, necessitating a jump of the bow in crossing the intervening string. This definition, used by Pincherle and La Laurencie in modern times, applies to passagework found in violin music as early as Rebel (French, 1713) and is described without any special term in the famous letter of Tartini to Maddalena Lombardini (1760).

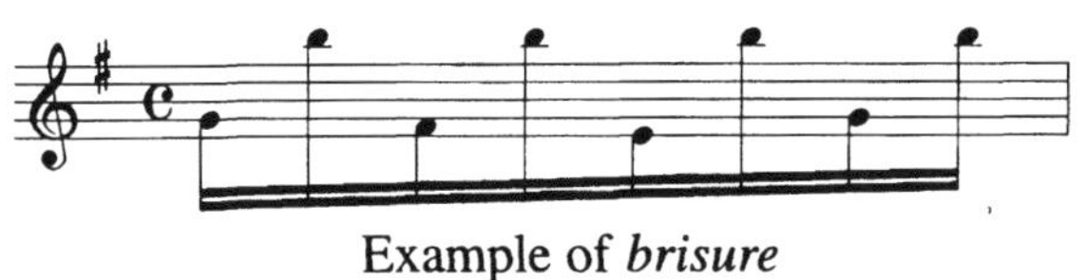

Example of *brisure*

brush stroke (E.) A type of *spiccato* bowing in which the horizontal motion is emphasized so that the bow drags or brushes the string and is lifted at the end of each stroke. This results in a more singing and less articulated bounce or lifted stroke than regular *spiccato*.

c. a. (It.) abbreviation for *coll'arco* (It.) With the bow. See *arco*.

calcare (It.) A bowing term used in the sixteenth century. Literally meaning "to crush," its technical meaning in violin playing is not known. (See Boyden, *History of Violin Playing*, 1965)

chapeau (F.) Slur sign. (Rousseau, *Dictionnaire de musique*, 1788)

chevalet (F.) Bridge.
    au __ At the bridge. See *ponticello*.
    en arrière du __ Play behind the bridge, between the tailpiece and
        bridge. See *behind the bridge*.
    près du __ Near the bridge. See *ponticello, poco sul ponticello*.
    sur le __ On the bridge. See *ponticello*.

col legno (It.) With the wood (of the bow). See *legno*.

collé (F.) Literally, "glued." A bowing in which the sound is produced by placing the bow on the string with a "light pinch" at the beginning of the stroke and immediately lifting it to prepare the next note. It is used as a practice bowing to develop full control of all parts of the bow, and may also be used as a substitute for a light *martelé* in fast tempi or to emphasize or slow down notes in spiccato passages. (Galamian, *Principles of Violin Playing and Teaching*, 1962). See *martelé, piqué, spiccato*.

16

colpo d'arco (It.) Bow-stroke.

concussion of notes (E.) A method of gracing notes described by Roger North (c. 1700). "And there is another way of gracing passing notes... It is as if every stroke were a mouthful and procured, as I take it, by... a sort of shock or concussion of the finger upon every touch, as if every note were torn ... from another; and this comprehends a very short mixture of every note with the next before or behind it, which fringes the tone, as colours are seen only at the entrance of a refraction." This produces an accented bowing, with the change of bow slightly before or after the forceful change of the finger. (North, "The Art of Gracing", c. 1700 in Wilson (ed.), *Roger North on Music*, 1959).

(notation of rhythm an approximation)
Example of *concussion of notes*

circular bowing (E.) A twentieth century term meaning a continuous sighing sound made by gradually gliding the bow away from the bridge on the down bow and over the fingerboard, then quickly returning the bow to the normal position on a light up bow to repeat the circular pattern.

contact point (E.) This refers to the point of contact of the bow hair on the string, that is, to the distance of the bow from the bridge, a crucial factor in the control of tone production. See *sounding point*.

continuato (It.) An eighteenth century term meaning notes sustained and continued with equal force, without shortening the sound or detaching the notes. The whole bow is used. (Brossard, *Dictionnaire de musique*, 1703).

corde, a la corda, alla corda (It.) On the string (following a passage played with bouncing bow-strokes).

    flatter la __ (F.) Caress the string. Expressive *son filé* or *legato* playing is implied.

    très à la __ (F.) Very *legato* or sustained.

coulé (F.) Slur. See *slur*.

coulement simple (F.) A slur to which no further ornamentation is to be added. (Muffat, *Florilegium Secundum*, 1698).

couler (F.) To slur. See *coulé, slur.*

coup d'archet (F.) Bow-stroke. See *articulé.*

craquer l'archet (F.) Two up-bows in succession, with a slight articulation between the notes and with the bow remaining on the string. This technique is used to make the bowing pattern conform to the "rule of the down-bow. (Muffat, *Florilegium Secundum*, 1698) See *rule of the down-bow.*

départ (F.) This term refers to a kind of bowing attack in which bow speed and pressure are constant at the beginning of and throughout horizontal motion of the bow stroke. An incisive attack will occur without sharp accentuation. (Galamian, *Basic Principles of Violin Playing and Teaching*, 1962).

détaché (F.) Comprises a family of bow-strokes, played on-the-string, which share in common a change of bowing direction with the articulation of each note. *Détaché* strokes may be sharply accentuated or unaccentuated, *legato* (only in the sense that no rest occurs between strokes), or very slightly *staccato*, with small rests separating strokes.

 accentuated __ A percussive attack, produced by great initial bow speed and pressure, characterizes this stroke. In contrast to the *martelé*, the *accentuated détaché* is basically a non-*staccato* articulation and can be performed at greater speeds than the *martelé* (generally used at the point). It is usually indicated only by accent marks.

 Franck, *Sonata in A Major* for Violin and Piano (last movement)

Example of *accented détaché*

 __ *lancé.* "Darting" *détaché.* Characteristically, a short unaccented *détaché* bow-stroke with some *staccato* separation of strokes. The marking shown in the example is that used by many modern teachers to indicate this bowing, although no marking at all is used in the original.

J.S. Bach, *Partita No. 2 for Violin Solo*, Ciaccona

Example of *détaché lancé*

court __ Short, separated, *détaché*.

__ *porté*. "Carried" *détaché*. This *détaché* stroke begins with a "slight swelling." (Galamian, *Principles of Violin Playing and Teaching*, 1962). Pressure is applied after horizontal motion begins and peak volume is reached shortly after soft initial attack. Release of pressure and, if desired, slight staccato separation from the next stroke follows. The bowing can provide expressive projection of musically important notes. It may be indicated by a horizontal dash, if any marking at all is used.

Tchaikovsky, *Violin Concerto in D Major*, Op. 35 (first movement)

Example of *détaché porté*

__ *rude*. See *accentuated détaché*.

grand __ Whole-bow *détaché* stroke.

large __ Same as grand *détaché*.

simple __ Most common of all bowings; unaccentuated, non-staccato *détaché*.

Historically:

In eighteenth century usage, *détaché* means separated.

detacher (F.) To play detached notes. See *détaché*.

dietro il ponticello (It.) See *behind the bridge*.

disjoindre (F.) To separate. See *detacher, détaché, spiccato*. (Brossard, *Dictionnaire de musique*, 1703).

distaccato (It.) Separated. (Tartini, letter to Maddalena Lombardini, 1760) See *staccato*.

down-bow (E.) When the bow-hand moves away from the instrument while bowing: Symbol = ⊓ (French symbol = ⊔).

down-bows, consecutive (E.) A bowing in which, for an effect of great strength, several notes are played by lifting and replacing the bow after each down-bow.

Tchaikovsky, Symphony No. 6, *"Pathétique"* (last movement)

Example of *consecutive down-bows*

drum stroke (E.) A thrown, rebounding bow stroke consisting of a series of consecutive pairs of *ricochet* articulations so that each bow stroke contains two rapid springing notes (alternating down and up bows). The stroke is done above the middle of the bow. Flesch considers it useful as a practice bowing for developing greater control. (Flesch, *The Art of Violin Playing*, 1924). This bowing is also known as *feather bowing* in the twentieth century.

Example of *drum stroke* bowing

effleurant la corde (F.) Late eighteenth century: Skimming over the surface of the string with a light bow.

Example of *effleurant la corde*

Erhebung des Bogens

Erhebung des Bogens (G.) Eighteenth century: Lifting of the bow for a lively expression. This is used for groups of two notes, as well as in larger groups, as shown below:

geschwinde Erhebung (rapid lifting of the bow)

Example of *Erhebung des Bogens*

Both *erheben* and *aufheben* are used in connection with groups of lifted notes in a single bow. *Abgestossen* is the general term for staccato used by German writers, but it does not describe the method by which the separation is produced. (Mozart, *Versuch einer gründlichen Violinschule*, 1756).

feather bowing

feather bowing (E.) See *drum stroke.*

festes staccato

festes staccato (G.) Firm or solid staccato. See *staccato.*

filer un son

filer un son (F.) To spin out a long tone. The earliest specific use of the term in connection with violin playing occurred in 1761 (L'Abbé le fils, *Principes du violon*, 1761). *Son filé* is described by L'Abbé le fils as a tone "sustained for a certain period at the same degree of force." By 1803, Baillot, Rode and Kreutzer (*Méthode de violon*) define it as a long tone with a swell and diminuendo. The term and effect are also found in vocal music; thus, in 1768 Rousseau defines it as including both meanings: "To manage the voice in such a way that one can prolong a sound without taking a new breath ... the first [method] is to sustain the note with equal strength on long notes; and the second is to make a crescendo, which is most used in passages and runs. The first is preferred by the Italians and the second by the French." (Rousseau, *Dictionnaire de musique*, 1768) See *son filé.*

firm staccato (E.) See *staccato* (No. 4).

flautando (It.) Literally "fluting or flute-like." An airy and breathy tone color obtained on a string instrument by drawing the bow lightly (light bow pressure ratio to bow speed) over the strings. *Flautando* does not mean "floating," and although usually played near or over the fingerboard, may also be played in other locations for various tonal effects. For example, *flautando quasi ponticello*; playing with a light bow stroke near the bridge produces a tonal variation of the *flautando* effect.

Berg, *Lyric Suite*

Example of *flautando*

flautato (It.) See *flautando*.

fliegendes staccato (G.) Flying staccato. See *staccato* (No. 5).

flying staccato (E.) See *staccato*. (No. 5).

fouetté (F.) Literally, "whipped." A sharply accentuated bowing performed, primarily, on an *up-bow* near the tip of the bow. The stroke can also be performed *down-bow*, at opportune moments, in lower areas of the bow. Characteristically, the bowing is usually performed following a down-bow *détaché* stroke. After the down-bow, the bow is lifted, when time permits, and struck back at once in a stinging, biting attack. The bow does not bounce off, but remains on the string. The stroke can simulate a martelé attack and can also assist the left hand in certain left-hand shifting situations.

Bruch, *Violin Concerto No. 1* in G Minor (first movement)

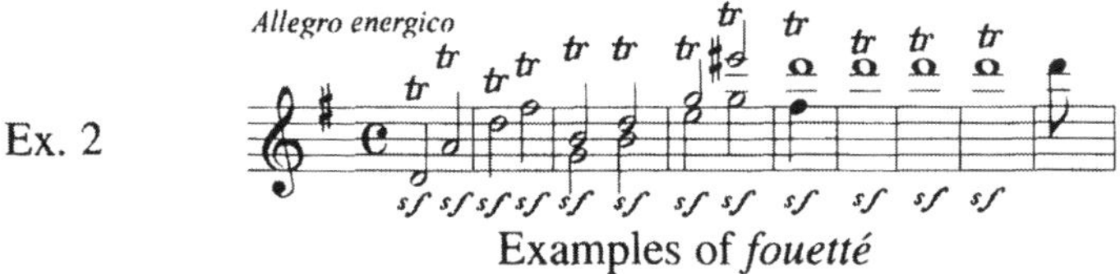

Ex. 2

Examples of fouetté

frappé avec l'archet (F.) Strike the string with the bow-stick. See *legno*. (Techniques 2).

frog (E.) A device made of ebony, ivory, tortoise-shell, etc. at the lower end of the bow to which the hair is fastened. A screw mechanism functions to adjust the tension of the hair by sliding the frog back and forth along the stick in the mortise.

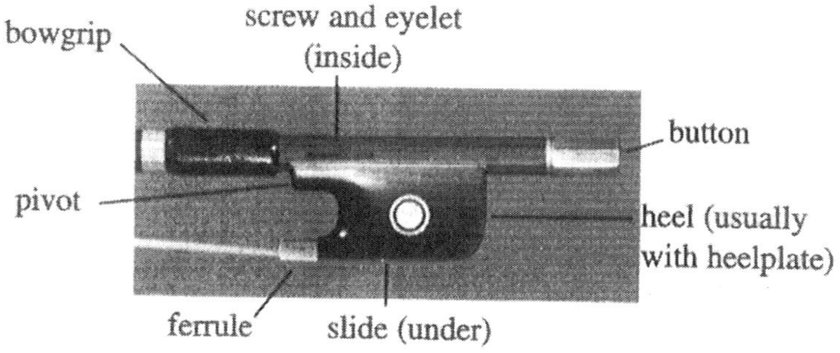

The Frog and its Component Parts

Frosch (G.) See *frog*.
   am __ At or near the frog.

frotté (F.) Rubbed.
   col legno __ The strings gently rubbed with the wood (stick) of the bow. See *legno*, col (Technique No. 6).

ganzer Bogen (G.) Whole bow. See *whole bow gliding*.

gebunden (G.) Slurred.

gehämmert (G.) See *martelé*.

gerissen (G.) Literally "torn" — pulled sharply. See *legno* (Techniques No. 9). Used by Webern in *Vier Stücke* for Violin and Piano.

geschlagen (G.) Hit or tapped. See *legno* (Techniques No. 2), *battuto, battu*.

gestossen (G.) Accentuated. Either *martelé* or accentuated *détaché*. See *abgestossen, martelé, détaché*.
   scharf __ Very accentuated.

gestrichen (G.) Drawn or bowed. Often used with *Holz* as in *mit Holz gestrichen* (G.) Drawn or bowed with the wood (stick). See *Holz, legno* (Techniques No.1), *tratto*.
   kurz __ Short bow-strokes.
   lang __ Long bow-strokes.

getrennt (G.) Separated bow-strokes.

gettato (It.) Thrown. See *jeté, ricochet*.

geworfener Strich (G.) Literally "thrown bow-stroke." See *jeté, ricochet, spiccato*.

gewöhnlich (G.) Usual, normal, ordinary, natural; used to indicate that the bowing is to change back to ordinary or normal playing, i.e., the basic violin tone produced in the normal way. For example, after a passage is marked *am Steg* (at the bridge), when the player is to resume the normal sound, "gewöhnlich" is indicated.
   wieder __ Again ordinary. See *ordinario, ordinaire, modo ordinario*.

grand détaché (F.) *Détaché* using the whole bow on each stroke. See *détaché*.

gezogen (G.) Sustained bowing style.
   lang __ Very sustained.

Griffbrett (G.) Fingerboard
   am __ See *tasto*.

guardate la legatura (It.) "Observe the slur." This warning is found in a Vivaldi concerto in connection with an unusual and interesting example of a bowing for a passage in Lombard rhythm:

Example of *guardate la legatura*

Example of *hair around the strings*

hair around strings (E.) An effect possible on string instruments accomplished by unscrewing the frog and separating it from the bow stick so that the player may wrap the loose hair around all four strings at once. In this technique, the bow stick is placed either underneath the body of a violin or viola or through the space underneath the strings between the bridge and the fingerboard of the cello and bass. The player then holds the unattached frog and the end of the frogless bow stick in the right hand so that the hair can be pulled back and forth over all four strings simultaneously. In this way, short, harmonium-like four note chords can be played. Single, double or triple stops cannot be sounded. Sustaining can only be approximated by changing bow direction. At best, this gimmick remains only a rare special effect.

harpeggiato, harpegiato, harpeggio (It.) harpége (F.) See *arpeggio*.

heel (E.) See *frog*.

Herabstrich, Herstrich, Herunterstrich (G.) Down-bow.

Heraufstrich, Hinstrich (G.) Up-bow.

Holz (G.) Wood (of the bow stick).
    mit ___; mit dem ___ zu streichen; with the wood; bow with the wood. See *legno* (Techniques No. 1).

jeté (F.) "Thrown." A series of consecutive up or down-bow *spiccato* strokes, each of which originates at the same point on the bow. Thus, in a series of up-bow bounces, the bow is lifted after each stroke and returned in the air to the point at which it began. The bow remains the same distance from the frog throughout the series of bounces. If the passage requires execution at a speed too fast to maintain the same bowing distance from the frog, the bow is permitted to creep in the bowing direction of the series. The difference between *jeté* and flying *staccato*, which also consists of a series of bounces in the same bowing direction, is that *jeté* is a considerably slower bowing, and that each bounce of the *jeté* is individually produced. The flying *staccato*, unlike the *jeté*, always creeps in the bowing direction of the series, and is produced in the manner of the firm *staccato*. Like the firm *staccato* to which it is related, flying *staccato* may have a trace of "bite" or sharp accentuation. See *staccato, ständiges* (No. 9).

Mendelssohn, *Violin Concerto in E Minor*, Op. 64 (last movement)

Examples of *jeté*

jeté col legno (F., It.) A drumstick-like effect in which the bow is thrown upon the string so that the wood of the bow stick ricochets or bounces.

lancé (F.). See *détaché lancé*.

legato (It.)
1) Bound together (literally, "tied"). Without interruption between the notes; smoothly connected, whether in one or several bows.
2) Sometimes explicitly means slurred, and is then indicated by a slur mark.

expressive or *inflected legato*. Slurred notes which are gently pulsed with bow pressure to bring them into expressive prominence. This bowing is often indicated by horizontal dashes under the slur, but this bowing can be used for expressive purposes when no marking occurs. When there is a very perceptible degree of pulsation or a separation in the sound, the bowing becomes a *louré* bowing. See *slur, louré*.

Wieniawski, *Violin Concerto in D Minor*, Op. 22 (Romanza)

Example of *inflected legato*

legatura (It.) Slur.

legno (It.) wood, *col legno* (It.) With the wood of the bow; to either draw the bow stick across the string or tap the string with the bow stick. In pure *col legno*, the bow hair is not used, but the edge of the hair can be allowed to contact the string along with the wood so that a more discernable pitch can be heard in the *col legno* tone color (notated as half *legno* or ½ *legno*). The earliest example of *col legno* is found in 1605 in *Musical Humors* by Tobias Hume, who instructs the performer to "drum this with the back of the bow." However, *col legno* remained a rare technique until the 20th century.

Col Legno Techniques
1) *col legno tratto, legno strisciato* (It.) *gestrichen* (G.) Drawing the wood over the string in legato style.
2) *col legno battuto* (It.) Hitting or tapping the string with the wood of the bow stick — a percussive effect. See *strike tone* for further discussion of *battuto*.
3) *half col legno - half arco* (E.) Drawing the bow so that both the wood and the hair are in contact with the string. This is accomplished by turning the bow on its side. With both the wood and hair in contact with the string, a clearer pitch results along with the scraping of the col legno.
4) *col legno battuto - sul tasto, sulla tastiera* (It.) Striking the strings directly over the fingerboard with the wood of the bow

(battuto) so that the sound of hitting the fingerboard — a violent, loud knocking is heard.

Bartók, *Sonata No.2 for Violin and Piano*

Example of *col legno battuto - sul tasto*

5) *col legno battuto - sul ponticello* (It.) Striking the strings directly upon the top of the bridge produces a loud knock.
6) *col legno frotté* (It., F.) The strings are gently rubbed with the wood of the bow.
7) *col legno - behind the bridge* (It., E.) String players may either tap the strings behind the bridge or draw the wood (stick) over the strings behind the bridge.
8) *col legno battuto - on the tailpiece or chinrest* (It., E.) String players may tap the tailpiece or the chinrest (on the violin or viola) with the wood (stick) of the bow.
9) *col legno gerissen* (It., G.) Pulled sharply ("torn") with accent over the string with the wood of the bow to produce a strong and dramatic *col legno* attack.

Webern, *Vier Stücke for Violin and Piano*, 1910

Example of *col legno gerissen*

10) *col legno weich gezogen* (It., G.) Drawn lightly with the bow stick.

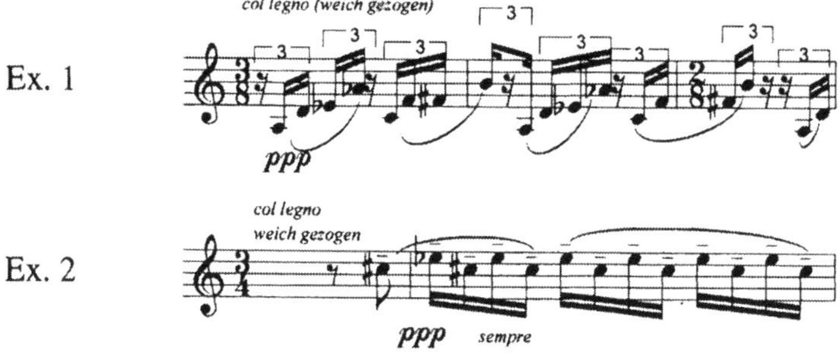

Examples of *col legno weich gezogen*

11) col legno jeté (It., F.) Bounced on the string with the bow stick.

In some more recent contemporary works, other ingenious experimental sounds produced by the wood of the bow have been used. Complete explanations of the method of performance are usually found rather than simply a new term. For example, the *String Quartet* by Roberto Gerhard uses *col legno* with:

1) Strings (as indicated) tapped *col legno* between bridge and tail-piece at varying spots, to produce varying series of random pitches and

2) Tapping *col legno* on the tailpiece, moving to and fro, from near the string towards the button.

lever l'archet (F.) Lift the bow.

liaison (F.) "Two or more notes on a single bow-stroke or ... marked by a curved line with which one covers the notes which are to be bound together." (Rousseau, *Dictionnaire de musique*, 1768).

libero (It.) Not slurred. "This is the contrary of *legato*. See *sciolto*." (Brossard, *Dictionnaire de musique*, 1703).

liées (F.) "One calls *notes liées* two or more notes which are made on a single bow-stroke..." (Rousseau, *Dictionnaire de musique*, 1768).

Ligatur (G.) Slur. (Kurzgefasstes musikalisches Lexikon, 1737).

lirate (It.) Slurred. (Usper, Compositione harmoniche, 1619).

lireggiare (It.) Slurred bowing using groups of notes from two to fifteen in number. (Rognoni, *Selva de varii passaggi secondo l'uso moderno*, 1620).

lireggiare affettuoso (It.) "The same as the above ..., but it is necessary that the motion of the bow arm beat every note as if it were skipping along (*saltellando*), one for one, and this is hard to do well; therefore this requires much study to be able to maintain the time in conformity with the value of the notes taking care not to make more noise with the bow than with the sound." (Rognoni, *Selva de varii passaggi secondo l'uso moderno*, 1620 — translation from Boyden, *The History of Violin Playing*, 1965) This is a unique instance of slurred, bounced *staccato* at such an early date, and it is marked in the music simply by the word *affeti* (ornaments). See *articulé, Erhebung des Bogens, jeté, ricochét and staccato.*

loosened bow hair (E.) A very soft, thin and distant sound created on a string instrument by using a bow with the hair tension unwound and slack.

louré (F.) This bowing consists of a short series of gently pulsed, slurred, *legato* notes. Varying degrees of articulation may be employed. The *legato* connection between notes may not be disrupted at all, but minimal separation may be employed. While the bow is in motion, pressure of the forefinger is applied to pulse a note, then released, and then reapplied for the following notes. This bowing is used in lyric passages to highlight expressive notes of a phrase. The range of articulation may be from a *legato* with a slight pressure on each note to gentle breaks in the sound. The marking for *louré* is usually a series of horizontal dashes under a slur, but dots may occasionally be found, as in the example below, which also uses the *louré* bowing in a very expressive pianissimo over the fingerboard. *Louré* is one of the bowing techniques employed in the *parlando* style when it is used in violin music. For early related bowings, see *tremolo* (historical meaning 1) and *tempered stoccata.* See *portato, parlando, tremolo, stoccato.*

Mendelssohn, *Violin Concerto in E Minor*, Op. 64
(first movement)

Ex. 1 

Sibelius, *Violin Concerto in D Minor*, Op. 47
(second movement)

Ex. 2 

Debussy, *Sonata for Violin and Piano* (first movement)**

Ex. 3 

Examples of *louré*

** Permission for reprint granted by Durand and Cie. Paris, France. Copyright owners-Elkan-Vogel Co. Inc. Philadelphia, Pa. Sole Agents.

markiert (G.) *Eighteenth Century*: Stressed; accented. This term does not indicate the degree or means of the stress, but merely some form of accent. According to Quantz in *Versuch einer Anweisung die Flute traversière zu spielen* (1752), the performer may use "either a short, light bow-stroke, or a heavy, sharp stroke."

martelé, marteler (F.), *martellando, martellato, martello*, (It.) *gehämmert* (G.) Hammered; a sharply accentuated, staccato bowing. To produce the attack, pressure is applied an instant before bow motion begins. The string is then very taut before it is set into vibration. The bow is thrust into motion with great initial speed, and pressure is simultaneously reduced. Tension is suddenly discharged as the string snaps into maximum amplitude with an explosive accent, characteristic of the stroke. The bow is then quickly stopped or lifted (at the frog) in order that there will be a silence before the next stroke. *Martelé* differs from the *accentuated détaché* in that the latter has primarily no *staccato* separation between strokes and can be performed at faster speeds.

Vieuxtemps, *Violin Concerto No. 4 in D Minor*, Op. 31
(fourth movement)

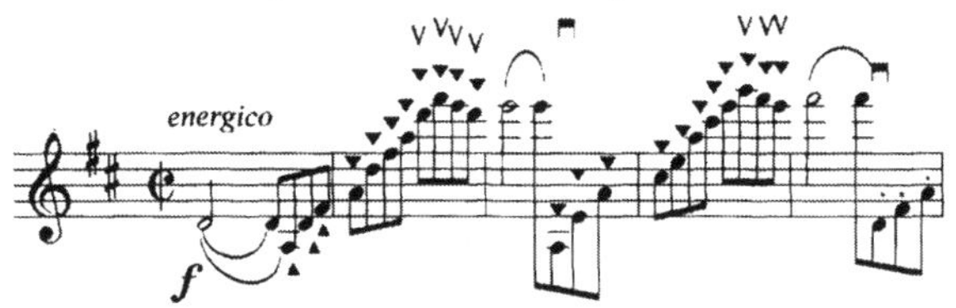

Example of *martelé*

__ chanté. "Singing" *martelé*. The *staccato* curtailment of bow-strokes is not as great as in martelé, yet greater than in the accented détaché.

Bruch, *Violin Concerto No.1 in G minor*, Op. 26 (first movement)

Example of *martelé chanté*

Historically:

Not used in connection with violin playing until sometime late in the eighteenth century. The earliest use of the term *martelé* in a modern sense in a method book is probably in 1800, though the stroke was certainly in use at least twenty-five years before this time. (Woldemar, *Grande méthode pour le violon*, 1800; *Le nouvel art de l'archet*, n.d.) In 1825, it was described as being executed at the point of the bow as had probably been the case in earlier use of the stroke. "This stroke [the *martelé*] must be executed at the point. It is necessary to attack each note sharply (*piquer chaque note*) as if to surprise the string quickly." (Baillot, Kreutzer, and Rode, *Méthode de violon*, 1825).

son *martelé* (F.) In the eighteenth century, a method of performing the note which follows the *port de voix* (an ornamental note which rises to the following principal note) in which the sound is augmented with the resolution to the principal note. "Taste requires that one

32

rest more or less long on the port de voix before expressing the note which follows it. It also demands very often that the note which follows the *port de voix be martelé* ... In the case of the *son feint* one diminishes the sonority but in the case of the *son martelé* one augments it." (L'Abbé le fils, *Principes du Violon*, 1761)

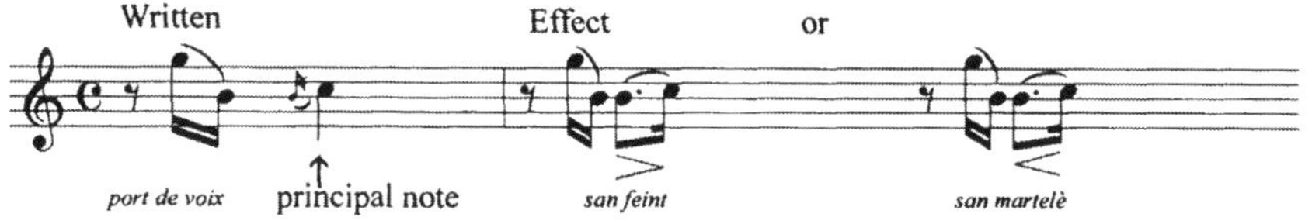

Example of *son martelé*

tremblement martelé (F.) In the seventeenth century, one of two types of trill (*tremblement*) described by Mersenne. *Tremblement martelé* is executed with separate strokes of the bow for each note of the trill; *tremblement non martelé* is a trill performed with one stroke of the bow, that is in *notes liées* (slurred notes). (Mersenne, *Harmonie universelle*, 1636-37) Though these terms are not in modern use, an effect related to the *tremblement martelé* is the modern *fingered tremolo détaché*. See *staccato, stabb.*

modo ordinario (It.) See *ordinario.*

natural (E.) *naturelle* (F.) In the ordinary, normal, usual manner. See *ordinario, gewöhnlich.*

Niederstrich (G.) See *down-bow.*

nicht tremolierend (G.) Non-*tremolo.* (Can also mean *non-vibrato*). See *tremolo.*

normal (E.) See *ordinario, gewöhnlich.*

nut (E.) See *frog.*

ondeggiando (It.) *ondulé* (F.) Undulating, moving in a wave-like motion.

1) Used in the seventeenth century to refer to a type of slurred *tremolo* on one string.
2) More commonly it refers to the slurred alternation between notes on two strings or a slurred *arpeggio* pattern crossing three or four strings. It is marked by a wavy line and a slur, or simply

by a slur. See *tremolo* (historical meaning No.1), *louré*, *bariolage*.

J. J. Walther, *Scherzi da violino solo*, 1676

Ex. 1 

Brahms, *Sonata No. 3 in D Minor*, Op. 108

Ex. 2 

Examples of *ondeggiando*

3) The same term is occasionally used to mean *vibrato*. (*Löhlein, Anweisung zum Violinspiel*, 1774).

ordinario (It.) *ordinary* (E.), *ordinaire* (F.) *gewöhnlich* (G.), *modo ordinario* (It.), *naturelle* (F.) *natural, normal* (E.). Used to indicate that the bowing is to change back to the normal, usual manner of playing after special bowing instructions were indicated, such as *col legno, sul ponticello, flautando* or *sul tasto.*

Bartók, *Violin and Piano Sonata* No.1

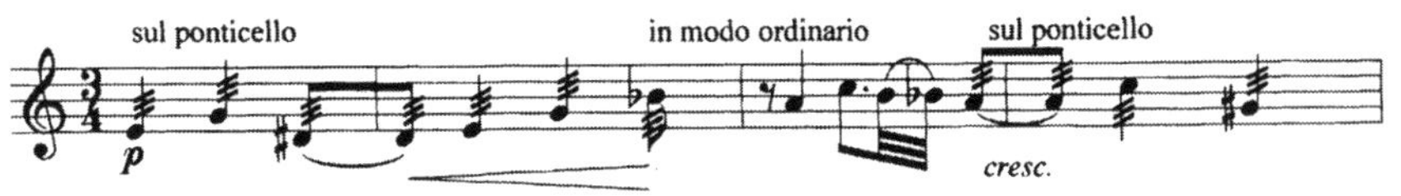

Example of *modo ordinario*

Paganini bowing (E.) A bowing pattern combining slurs and *détaché* in the combination shown below.

Paganini, *Caprice No. 16*

Example of *Paganini bowing*

parlando (It.) Expressive, declamatory, almost recitative-like style of playing. It may use a variety of expressive bowings, such as the *louré* or the *détaché porté*.

Bartók-Szigetti, *Hungarian Folktunes* No.1

Example of *parlando*

pedal tones (E.) A phrase coined by George Crumb in *Black Angels for Electric String Quartet* to describe notes produced on a string which vibrate (and sound) actually lower than the open string. This is accomplished (usually on the lowest string) by excessive bow pressure and very slow bow speed upon the string and by placing the bow near or over the fingerboard where the string is loose. In this way a type of pitched noise is produced sounding an octave lower than the note being fingered or the open string itself. This effect is difficult to achieve successfully and at best can only be used for an unusual tonal event.

perlé, coup d'archet (F.) A term derived from lute playing and meaning brilliant and delicate (*Furetière, Dictionnaire universel*, 1701). As applied to violin bowing in the later eighteenth century, it meant a series of articulated notes in one bow, which may be either up-bow or down-bow (although up-bow was easier and more commonly used). See *articulé*.

Bornet, *Nouvelle Méthode de Violon*, 1786

Example of *perlé*

picchettato (It.) A general term for off-the-string bowings which may also be used as a synonym for *piqué*. Also the Italian term for *firm staccato* (a *sautillé* that does not leave the string, but sounds as if the bow is rebounding).
 __ balzato. See *jeté*.

___ saltellato. See *drum-stroke.*

___ volante. Italian term for the staccato volante (*flying staccato*).

Historically:

Eighteenth Century: Articulated notes on one bow stroke (Le Duc, *6 Sonates pour le violon*, circa 1760). Lichtental, however, in the early nineteenth century, translated *picchettato* as *piqué.* (Lichtental, *Dictionnaire de musique*, translated and augmented by Mondo, 1839).

piqué (obs. spelling, *picqué*) (F.) Literally "pricked" or "spurred." A type of bowing which possesses the accentuated attack of the *martelé* with the bow immediately lifted from the string following the attack. As a result of the lifted release, *piqué* can be performed far more softly and more *staccato* than *martelé.* See *collé, piquer.*

piquer (F.)

Historically:

1) To separate; to make "each note be heard distinctly." (Tans'ur, *A New Musical Grammer,* 1748) "Almost the same" as *staccato, stoccato, or spiccato,* for which see the historical meanings. (Brossard, *Dictionnaire de musique,* 1703). To shorten with the bow. (Dard, *Nouveaux principes de musique,* 1769). These definitions do not imply that the bow leaves the string.

2) A manner of playing by dotting [that is, placing staccato dots ⋅ above or below the notes] and strongly marking the dot. *Notes piquées* are groups of notes rising or descending diatonically or repeated on the same degree, on each of which one sets a dot, sometimes a little elongated [that is, a dash ⸳] to indicate that they ought to be marked equally by the strokes of the bow, dry and detached (*secs et détachés*), without retaking the down-bow or up-bow, but making it go by striking and jumping on the string (*frappant et sautant sur la corde*)." (Rousseau, *Dictionnaire de musique,* 1768). This is the earliest definition in which this particular word, which is the French equivalent of the Italian word *spiccato* is explicitly described as using a bouncing bow. Earlier definitions do not specify the means by which the notes are to be shortened, and the common method of performance in the earlier eighteenth century was probably on the string for such a succession of shortened notes. See *spiccato.*

pikieren (pikiren) (G.) See *piquer* (No. 2). To play with a rapid, detached stroke, "which belongs more to the soloist than to the *ripieno* player." (Hiller, *Anweisung zum Violinspielen*, 1795).

pitched noise (E.) An unusual tonal effect on a stringed instrument resulting from increasing bow pressure upon the string while decreasing bow speed so that the normal clear tone takes on more or less noise (scratchiness or raspiness). In pitched noise, the pitch is always discernible no matter how much noise is present in the sound. See *scratch, noise*.

pointe (F.) Bow-tip.
> *à la* ___ At the bow-tip.
> *à la* ___ *comme col legno*. Tap at the bow-tip with the hair flat in the style of *col legno*.
> *avec la* ___ At the bow tip.
> *de la* ___ At the bow-tip.
> *vers la* ___ Toward the bow-tip.

pointer (F.)
1) "Signifies to separate or divide each note from another in a very plain and distinct manner." (Bailey, *Dictionarium Britannicum*, 1730). Pointer may also mean to write a note with a dot. The dot may be a staccato mark, above or below the note. "The dotted note must be accented and the bow must be detached (*abgesetzet* [lifted?] in the German edition; *détaché* in the French edition) for the value of the dot." (Quantz, *Versuch einer Anweisung die Flute traversière zu spielen*, 1752; *Essai d'une méthode pour apprendre à jouer de la flute traversière*, 1752). See *staccato* and *spiccato*. (Brossard, *Dictionnaire de musique*, 1703).
2) More commonly, to make unequal notes which are notated equally (*notes inégales*). "Eighth notes are not always played equally, and ... in some measures there ought to be a long one and a short one; this is determined by their number. When this is even, the first is taken long, the second short, and so forth. When it is an odd number, the opposite pattern is followed. This is called *pointer*." (Hotteterre, *Principes de la flûte traversière*, 1707). "We play as dotted (*pointer*) a succession of eighth notes in conjunct motion and yet we write them as equal." (Couperin,

L'art de toucher le clavecin, 1717). To make more unequal notes which are already dotted. " ... one makes the first half-beat much longer than the second, but the first half-beat ought to be dotted. This is called *Piquer*, or *Pointer*." (Loulié, *Elements ou principes de musique*, 1696).

Note that when *pointer* means *staccato*, it does not mean unequal; when it means to make equally notated notes unequal in performance, it has no specific implications with respect to the method of articulation; and when it means the exaggerated performance of a notated dotted rhythm, it is likely to be performed with a silence before the short note of the pattern.

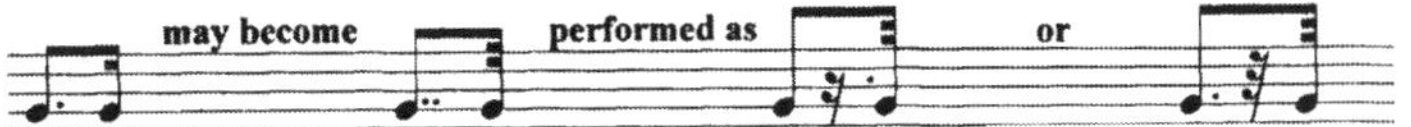

pointiller (F.) *Eighteenth Century*: To make rapid short notes with a springing bow. "Gay music puts dots on the notes to make them shorter (*pointiller les notes*), and makes the sounds jump (*sautiller*); the bow is always in the air"... (Chabanon, *De la musique considérée en elle-même*, 1785). See *sautillé* (historical meaning).

pontare (It.) To play up-bow.

ponticello, *sul ponticello* (It.); *Steg, am Steg* (G.); *puentecillo, sobre el puentecillo* (Sp.); *chevalet, sur le chevalet* (F.) Bridge; on or upon the bridge. A special *tone color* on a string instrument produced by bowing very close to or upon the bridge, so that the pitch becomes weak or even unrecognizable and the raspy, nasal upper partials dominate. In pure *sul ponticello*, the bow hair is right at the bridge and the pitches are not identifiable. Should pitch recognition be musically desirable, the bow hair is placed somewhat away from the bridge. Composers use terms like *poco* or *half (1/2) sul ponticello* when pitches should be recognized in the special tone color. *Sul ponticello* as a marking first appears in a violin composition by Farina in 1627 (*Capriccio Stravagante*), but was not used again until the time of Boccherini. In 20th century music, *sul ponticello* is an often used tone color in string compositions.

al __ At the bridge.

dietro il __ See *behind the bridge, tone color.*

Example of *sul ponticello*

portamento (It.) An expressive slide from one pitch to another, **not** a legitimate bowing term. It has sometimes been used **mistakenly** to mean *portato* or *louré*. See *portato, louré*.

portato (It.), *porté* (F.) Notes played in one bow-stroke which are articulated without lifting the bow from the string. They are neither slurred *legato* nor detached but almost connected. (Lichtental, *Dictionnaire de musique*, 1839). The term *portato* was not used to mean a violin-bowing until the end of the eighteenth century; however, the meaning Lichtental gives corresponds to the slurred form of the *tremolo* and the modern *louré* bowing. See *tremolo, louré*.

poussé (F.) Up-bow.

pousser (F.) To play up-bow.

puentecillo (Sp.) Bridge.
   sobre el __. On the bridge. See *ponticello*.

punktieren (punktiren) (G.) See *pointer*.

punta, *punto* (It.) Bow-tip.
   a punta d'arco. At the bow-tip.
   colla __. At the bow-tip.
   __ *d'arco, quasi col legno*. Tap at the bow-tip simulating *col legno*.
   colla __ *d'arco*. At the bow-tip.
   __ *dell'arco*. At the bow-tip.
   sulla __. At the bow-tip.
   __ *d'arco*. "Notes marked with these words demand a particular
      execution, which consists of striking gently (*doucement*) on the
      string *with the tip of the bow* one produces thus a very lively
      staccato." (Lichtental, Dictionnaire de musique, 1839)
   al punto. At the bow-tip.
   col __ *del arco*. At the bow-tip.
   coll' __. At the bow-tip.

rebound, *recovery* (E.) A term coined by Paul Rolland (*Basic Principles of Violin Playing*, 1959) to describe the bowing motion of full *recovery*; "The bow is moved and returned in the air to the point of origin."

Lalo, *Symphonie Espagnole*, Op. 21 (first movement)

Example of *rebound* or *recovery*

reprise d'archet (F.) The return of the bow to the frog for the successive *down-bows* called for in certain contexts by the *rule of the down-bow* in seventeenth and eighteenth century bowing practice. (Muffat, *Florilegium Secundum*, 1698). See *rule of the down bow*.

ricochet (F.) A series of two or more slurred and, characteristically, very fast bounces, usually performed in the upper-half of the bow. The bow is dropped or struck upon the string in such a way that the initial impetus and natural elasticity of the bow gives rise to a spontaneous series of successive bounces.

Dont, *24 Etudes and Caprices*, Op. 35, No. 4

Ex. 1
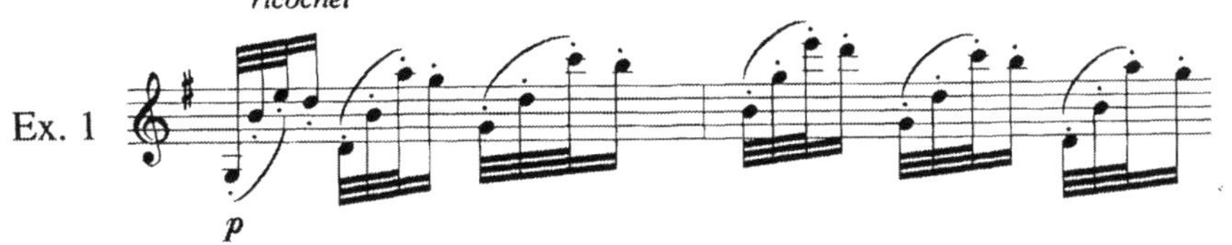

Rossini, *Overture to William-Tell*

Ex. 2

Examples of *ricochet*

Historically:

Bouncing bow, perhaps similar to the modern *spiccato*. Unfortunately the source in which this term first appears does not describe it except as an effect in "passages from high to low or low to high with bow strokes called *Ricochets*." The writer, a viol-player, does not approve of their use, and regards them as scarcely bearable even on the violin. Unfortunately no violinist of the day described them nor is the term found elsewhere. It is possible that the author is referring to *arpeggio* passages. (Jean Rousseau, *Traité de la Viole*, 1687). See *arpeggio (springing)*, *spiccato*.

rotary motion (bowing) (E.) See *circular bowing*.

roulé (F.) A practice routine to develop suppleness in the right hand fingers and to develop good tone production. The bow-stick is rolled by the fingers while drawing sustained bow-strokes so that the stick gradually and continuously changes the direction in which it faces, from fingerboard to bridge.

rule of the down-bow (E.) In early violin-playing, the rule is that a down-bow should be used on the first beat of each measure unless the measure begins with a rest. The up-bow is to be used on unaccented notes. In the event that there is an uneven number of notes in the measure, as is likely to be the case in triple time, the bowing may be either,

with successive down-bows requiring a *reprise d'archet* between the

measures, or

with two consecutive up-bows and no *reprise d'archet.*

The successive up-bows are clearly articulated and called *craquer* by Muffat. (Muffat, *Florilegium Secundum*, 1698). The rule of the down-bow is considered basic by all writers, from Mersenne (*Harmonie universelle*, 1636-37) to Mozart (*Versuch einer gründlichen Violinschule*, 1756), though in actual practice such a restrictive system was often departed from. Geminiani, indeed, strongly inveighs against the rule: "taking Care not to follow that wretched Rule of drawing the Bow down at the first Note of every Bar." (Geminiani, *The Art of Playing on the Violin*, 1751).

The rule seems to have been followed most closely and to have had the most musical value in the seventeenth century French dance style where it resulted in clearly accented and articulated dance rhythms, closely associated with the actual step patterns. Muffat, describing for German readers what we assume to have been the Lully code of bowing practice for French orchestral violinists of the seventeenth century, illustrates the basic principle with the following minuet:

Bracketed two measures are one length of the step-pattern.

Note that the *reprise d'archet* occurs only between step patterns, where its high degree of separation serves to mark the phrase, and that measures within the pattern use successive up-bows (*craquer*). See *craquer, reprise d'archet.*

saltato, saltando, saltante (It.) Bounced, bouncing. All the terms derived from *saltare* (to jump) have the general meaning of bouncing bows. They may have particular reference to a grouped bouncing stroke (such as *jeté* or *ricochet*) but this usage is not consistent. Example 1 might also be called *ricochet* or *jeté*; example 2, *flying staccato*. See *spiccato, jeté, ricochet, sautillé, staccato*.

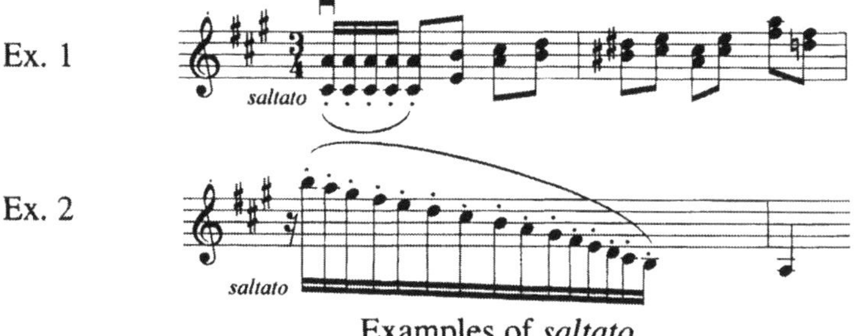
Dancla, *20 Brilliant and Characteristic Etudes*, Op. 73, No. 14

Examples of *saltato*

saltellando (It.) With skipping or jumping bow; a term used by Rognoni (1620) to describe the performance of a succession of bounced *staccati* in one bow. Though this is an extremely early, isolated use of the term, a similar stroke is suggested by such terms in common eighteenth century use as *coup d'archet articulé, Erhebung des Bogens* (particularly *geschwinde Erhebung*) and *coup d'archet perlé. Coup d'archet articulé* or *perlé*, however, may be either on or off the string, and neither the term nor the notation specifies which method of performance is to be used. Passages which could use either are found in the works of such virtuosi as Locatelli and Veracini. See *lireggiare affettuoso, articulé, perlé, Ehrebung des Bogens*.

sautillé (F.) *Erhebung des Bogens* (G.) *perlé, coup d'archet* (F.) A characteristically rapid, and alternating down and up-bow bouncing stroke. When executed at the correct bouncing point, the resilience of the bow stick is brought into play and the bow springs off the string. The *sautillé* is similar to the rapid *détaché* stroke, but whereas the sautillé jumps off the string, the *détaché* remains firmly on the string. The *sautillé* is often indicated by dots.

Haydn, *String Quartet in D Major*, Op. 64, No. 5 (last movement)

Example of *sautillé*

*Note: There are no dots in the Haydn Urtext, although some editors

add them and most string quartets play this passage off the string.
Historically:

With bouncing bow. It was first defined in connection with violin bowing by Piani as indicating "equal notes, articulated and a little detached (*notes égales, articulées et un peu détachées*)." Although the first use of this term occurs in French, Piani was an Italian violinist living in Paris, and was very likely using a translation of a term and technique already in existence in Italian violin playing. This is the earliest use of a term which clearly refers to separate bouncing bow strokes, though Jean Rousseau's use of *ricochet* might imply such a stroke. (Jean Rousseau, *Traité de la Viole*, 1687). Piani marks the notes to be played *sautillé* with dots. They are eighth notes, and the performance would be like modern *spiccato*. (Piani, *Sonate a violino solo e violoncello col cimbalo*, op. 1, 1712).

schleiffen, *schleiffeln* (G.) To slur. The German noun *Schleifer* (*Schleiffer, Schleiffung*) is a slurred ornament filling in the interval of the third. (Ahle, *Anleitung der Singekunst*, 1690.) Quantz, however, gives several examples of different bowing patterns mixing slurred and detached notes, as well as a wide variety of dynamic patterns for the *Schleifer*. (Quantz, *Versuch einer Anweisung die Flute traversière zu spielen*, 1752). See *coulé, slur*.

scratch (E.) An unpitched *noise* produced on a string instrument by excessive bow pressure and very slow bow speed. Although scratching on a string instrument was religiously avoided as a musical sound before the twentieth century, it is occasionally requested by some modern composers as a special effect and *tone color*. It can be used as one type of *noise* dissonance that resolves to pitch consonance. See *noise, pitched noise, pedal tones, tone color*.

sec, coup d'archet (F.) "Dry bow stroke." (Brossard, *Dictionnaire de musique*, 1703). See *spiccato, staccato* (Historical meanings).

separer les sons (F.) "To separate the sounds." See *spiccato, staccato, tronco* (Brossard, *Dictionnaire de musique*, 1703).

slur (E.) A curved line grouping notes together. In string music, those notes included by a slur are played in the same bowing direction, either all up-bow or all down-bow. The notes are played *legato* unless additional marks, such as dots or dashes under the slur indicate separation by stopping, lifting, or bouncing the bow. See *Bindung, chapeau* (slur sign), *coulé, coulement simple, gebunden, legatura, liaison, liées, ligatur, lirate*, and *lireggiare*, for terms dealing with *legato* slurs. For separated bowings grouped in a single bow, see *louré, articulé, perlé, craquer, Erhebung des Bogens, tremolo* (historical meaning No.1), *jeté, staccato* (historical meaning), *flying staccato*, and *ricochet*.

slurred staccato (E.) See *staccato* (No. 2).

smorzato (It.) "Bear a light Bow, and play soft." (Tan'sur, *A New Musical Grammar*, 1746). "Means such a bow-stroke that the sound of the instrument (becomes) always weaker and weaker." (Walther, *Musikalisches Lexikon*, 1732). "Intimates that the Bow or Fiddle-stick be drawn to its full length, and that not with the same strength of hand throughout, but bearing lighter and lighter on it by degrees, 'till scarce any sound be heard." (Grassineau, *A Musical Dictionary*, 1740).

son filé (F.) Literally, "spun tone." This term refers to a slow sustained, singing bowing style employed in performing lyric, expressive passages. Most often, the bow will be used quite close to the bridge with a high ratio of bow pressure to bow speed. See *filer un son.*

Brahms, *Violin Sonata No. 3 in D Minor*, Op. 108
(second movement)

Adagio

Example of *son filé*

sounding point (E.) The term used for the best place on the string in relation to the bridge for bow contact to produce the desired focused tone. (Galamian, *Principles of Violin Playing and Teaching*, 1962). See *contact point.*

sostenuto (It.) Played in a sustained manner. See *soutenir*.

soutenir (F.) *Eighteenth century*:
1) To hold the note for its full value without releasing before the end of the note. (Rousseau, *Dictionnaire de musique*, 1768).
2) To sustain a sound without nuance. (L'Abbé le fils, *Principes du violon*, 1761, in which it is used to define the *son filé*). See *son filé, sostenuto*.

spiccato (It.)
1) Refers to a slow to moderate speed bouncing stroke. Every degree of crispness is possible in the *spiccato*, ranging from gently brushed to percussively dry. *Spiccato* can be played as fast as a slow *sautillé*, but beyond a certain speed, becomes impractical.
2) Also used as a generic term meaning any speed of alternating down and up-bow bouncing strokes.

(Brahms, *Trio in B Major*, Op. 8)

(Beethoven, *String Quartet in C# Minor*, Op. 131)

Examples of *spiccato*.

semi spiccato See *brush stroke*.

flying spiccato A series of rapid *spiccato* notes played on one bow stroke, with each note individually activated, similar to the *flying staccato*. See *brush stroke, sautillé, staccato*.

Historically:

"From the verb *spiccare*, which is to say, to separate (*séparer, disjoindre*). This [*spiccato*] is an Italian [word which means] ... that it is necessary to detach or separate the sounds well from each other (*détacher ou séparer les sons*)." (Brossard, *Dictionnaire de musique*, 1703). Though this is an eighteenth century definition, the word appears as a musical term as early as the sixteenth century. It means separation of sounds only and does not describe the means or degree of the separation. It does **not** have the modern meaning of bouncing bow until the nineteenth century, and even as late as 1811 it was still being defined in dictionaries as meaning merely the separation of sounds. "A word denoting that the notes over which it is placed are to be performed in a distinct and pointed manner." (Busby, *A Complete Dictionary of Music*, 1789, edition of 1811). In the later eighteenth century, there is more emphasis in the definitions on the dryness of the sound. "*Spiccato* ... indicates dry and well detached sound (*sons secs et bien détachés*)." (Rousseau, *Dictionnaire de musique*, 1768).

The early *spiccato* is indicated by dots, by vertical dashes, by the word itself, or is left to the judgement of the performer. When the word is used, it usually appears in slow movements as part of the tempo indication: *Largo molto e spiccato* (Vivaldi, PV 290). "*Spiccato* (or *staccato*), is to say that the bow-strokes should be played dryly, without being connected and well detached. This is very often found in the *Largo* and *Adagio* of the Concerto." (Corrette, *L'école d'Orphée*, 1738).

Spitze (G.) Bow-tip.
>*an der ___ des Bogens*. At the bow-tip.
>an der ___ *gestrichen*. Bowed at the tip.
>*___ des Bogens, wie col legno*. Tap at the bow-tip in simulation of *col legno*.

Springbogen, *springend* (G.) Bouncing bow. See *spiccato, sautillé, jeté, ricochet*.

springing arpeggio (E.) See *arpeggio*.

stabb, *stab* (G.) See *stoccato, abgestossen*.

staccato (It.)

1) Used as a generic term, *staccato* means a non-legato *martelé* type of short bow-stroke played with a stop. The effect is to shorten the written note value with an unwritten rest.

Composers often use this term in its generic sense.

2) In modern violin playing *staccato* is specifically a series of
slurred martelé strokes characteristically performed in the upper
half of the bow. Each stroke may be produced at a relatively
slow speed in the manner of the *martelé*, where an individual
effort must be made to attack and release each note. A considerably
faster *staccato* may be obtained by other means, but the
rate of speed is not as easy to control. This is called *flying staccato*.
To avoid confusion with the **generic** meaning of *staccato*,
the terms *slurred staccato* or *group staccato* may be used. It has
been suggested that the on-the-string *staccato* bowings be classified
according to their speed as follows: *slurred staccato*
(medium speed), *martelé staccato* (slow), and *rapid staccato.*

3) *Staccato* may also refer to a style of bowing which may be
likened to an unaccentuated *martelé*. The bow is not pressed
before motion begins. Thus no sharp report, as in *martelé*, but a
soft, "round" attack is produced. The bow is moved very rapidly
and stopped abruptly to provide a rest before the next stroke
begins.

4) *firm (or solid) staccato* (E.), *festes Staccato* (G.) As in *staccato*
(No.2) *firm staccato* also consists of slurred *martelé* articulations,
but can be performed at much faster, although mostly
involuntary, rates of speed capable of little regulation. This is
because the *staccato* stroke (No. 2) requires an individual application
and release of pressure to produce each articulation,
whereas the *firm staccato* requires reflexive, spasmodic muscular
motions—the bow being firmly pressed into the string
throughout the slurred series and the reflexive motion itself provides
the attacks and separations. The reflex motions employed
by performers are of two basic kinds. One is related to the oscillating
motion of the wrist as used to perform a rapid *tremolo*.
The other is related to the spasmodic motion of the arm. See
martelé, flying staccato.

Example of the *firm staccato*

5) *flying staccato* (E.), *fliegendes Staccato* (G.), *staccato volante* (It.), *staccato volant* (F.) A series of fast up-bow slurred, bouncing strokes, characteristically performed in the upper half of the bow. This bowing is very much akin to the *firm staccato*, in that it is produced by a series of rapid reflex motions. In contrast to the *firm staccato*, the strokes are lighter, far less sharply accentuated, and, for the most part, bounce off the string. See *jeté*.

Berg, *Violin Concerto*

Example of *flying staccato*

6) *geworfenes Staccato* (G.) See *ricochet*.
7) *martelé* __ See *No.1 above*.
8) __ *jeté* (F.) See *ricochet*.
9) __ *mordant* (F.) See *firm staccato*. See No. 4 above.
10) *ständiges* __ (G.) "Standing" *staccato*. A succession of thrown up-bows at the same point on the bow. See *jeté*. (Flesch, *The Art of Violin Playing*, 1924).
11) __ *sautillant* (F.) Ricochet strokes of from two to four bounces, each consecutively following one another to produce a continuous stream of fast bouncing articulations. See *ricochet, drum stroke*.

Historically:

Detached. "*Staccato* ... is almost the same as *spiccato*, namely that the bow-strokes must be short, without connection, and well separated from each other." (Walther, *Musikalisches Lexikon*, 1732). The term *staccato* is, of course, in common use through the entire seventeenth century. It does not describe the means or degree of separation, and it has no special technical meaning for any particular instrument, as it was later to acquire for the violin. It is often listed as synonymous with *spiccato*, as indeed the two verbs **staccare** and **spiccare** were listed as synonyms in general Italian dictionaries. (*Vocabolario degli Accademici della Crusca*, 1623). A typical definition in a musical dictionary is that of Brossard: "*Staccato* or *Stoccato*, is almost the same thing as *spiccato*. That is to say that, on all the bowed instruments, they ought to make their bow-strokes dry (*secs*), without connection, and well detached (*détachez*) or separated (*séparez*) the one from the other, that is almost what we call in French, *picqué* or *pointé*." (Brossard, *Dictionnaire de musique*, 1703). *Staccato* is typically described as shortening the note by half its value: "*Staccato*, that is, separate and detached ... should be played as if there were a rest after every note." Tartini, letter to Maddalena Lombardini, 1760, trans. Burney, 1771.

notated   performed

Like *spiccato*, *staccato* is found combined with tempo indications, usually for slow movements, (for example, *Largo e staccato*, in Veracini, *Sonate accademiche a violin solo*, Op. 2, 1744). On the other hand, Roger North refers to "merry" pieces (probably fast) as *staccatas*: "He [John Jenkins] would be often in a merry humour; and make catches, and some strains he called Rants, which were like our *staccatas*." (North, "Memoires of Musick," 1728, in Wilson (ed.), *Roger North on Music*, 1959).

Some descriptions of *staccato* in the eighteenth century instruct the violinist to lift the bow, although this was by no means always included in the meaning of the term. The lifted bow may be a single note or a succession of notes. Muffat uses a lifted bow to end a suspension, in his *concerti* in Italian style and refers to this as *staccato*. (*Ausserlesene mit*

50

Ernst und Lust gemengte Instrumentalmusik, 1701). Geminiani uses the term *staccato* for a succession of lifted or off-the-string bows: "*Staccato*, where the Bow is taken off the Strings at every note." However, he considers this a good practice only for eighth notes in *allegro*, and describes this type of *staccato* as "bad or for a particular effect" in adagio or andante movements. It is regarded as bad in sixteenth-notes in fast tempi. (Geminiani, *The Art of Playing on the Violin*, 1751). By 1770, Hoyle defines *staccato* as requiring the bow to be lifted for every note. (Hoyle, *Dictionarium Musica*, 1770). See *abgezucht, abgesetzet, abgestossen, articulation, articuler, aufgehoben, détaché, disjoindre, distaccato, Erhebung des Bogens, lireggiare affettuoso, piquer, pointer, ricochet, saltellando, saltato, sautillé, sec, séparer les sons, spiccato, stoccata (stoccato), stab (stabb), and tronco.*

Steg (G.) Bridge.

 am __ At the bridge. See *ponticello.*
 auf dem __ On the bridge. See *ponticello.*
 hinter dem __ A special bowing effect. Play in back of the bridge
  between the bridge and the tailpiece. See *behind the bridge.*
 nahe zum __ Near the bridge. See *ponticello.*
 zum __ To the bridge. See *ponticello.*

stoccato (stoccata) (It.) An eighteenth century synonym for *staccato.*

There are, however, two references to the term which indicate a possible difference in some aspects of the meaning. Walther points out that *stoccato* is not derived from a verb meaning to detach (as *staccato* is), but from the word for rapier (*stocco*), and thus means "*gestossen* (stabbed or pounded), *nicht gezogen* (not drawn out)." (Walther, *Musicalisches Lexikon*, 1732). Roger North, writing at almost the same time, describes the *stoccato* as a violent stroke belonging to the Italian style of playing as practiced by Nicolai Matteis: "Another grace, or rather manner, is the *Stoccata* or stabb, which is a peculiar art of the hand upon instruments of the bow. And as it is an occasional imitation, so it hath a due acceptance; but to use it at all turns, whensoever the movement will allow it, creates a *fastidium*. For it doth not ... mend the harmony, but rather by an affected snatching deprive it... Old Signor Nichola Matteis used this manner to set off a rage, and then a repentance; for after a violent *stoccata*, he entered at once with a bipedalian [two foot long] bow, as speaking no less in a passion, but of the contrary temper." (Roger North, "The Art of Gracing", c. 1700 in Wilson (ed.), *Roger North on Music*, 1959). North's description implies a single strongly accented stroke, perhaps a forerunner of the modern *martelé* which ends abruptly. It seems that it was not to be used, however, for a succession of short, accented notes. For most eighteenth century writers, however, *stoccato* is treated as if it were merely another spelling of *staccato*.

tempered stoccata (E.) See *tremolo* (historical meaning No.1). North describes it as follows: "There is another mode of the *Grave* that frequently occurs in our Italianized sonatas, which I have known intituled *Tremolo*, and is now commonly performed with a tempered *stoccata*. And that I take to be an abuse, and contrary to the genius of that mode, which is to hold out long notes enriched with the flowers of harmony and with a trembling hand [bow *tremolo*] which of all parts together resembles the shaking stop of an organ; whereas the breaking of the notes with repeated strokes doth not well consist with the best of harmony." Though North does not approve of the tempered *stoccata*, this passage indicates that an articulated bow stroke, performed on the string, was associated with the Italian style in early eighteenth century England. (North, *"The Common Characters of Musick," The Musicall Grammarian*, 1728, in Wilson (ed.), *Roger North on Music*, 1959). See *staccato, tremolo, stabb.*

strappato (It.) Torn off; sharply accented. Used by Vivaldi (*La Primavera*) for a passage in which the viola is to imitate a barking dog, "molto forte, e strappato," by means of a vigorous attack and rough release.

Vivaldi, *La Primavera Concerto*

Il cane che grida. Si deve suonare sempre molto forte, e strappato.
"The dog which barks. It ought to sound always very loud and torn off."

Example of *strappato*

stricciate (It.) Used by Vivaldi to describe the performance of repeated thirty-second notes. Boyden believes it is related to the verb *streccia-*

re (untwist, divide), but it might possibly come from *strisciare* (touch slightly) and be a type of light *sautillé*.

Strich (G.) Bow-stroke.
> *geworfener* __ Literally "thrown bow-stroke." See *jeté, ricochet, spiccato*.
> *mit breitem* __ With broad or full bow-strokes.
> *Stricharten* Styles of bowing.
> *Strich für* __ Non-slurred; change bow direction with each note.
> *grosser* __ Whole-bows.

strike tone (E.) A soft, high pitched click heard in addition to the louder, actual sound produced when tapping the string with the wood of the bow known as *col legno battuto*. The strike tones are heard simultaneously as part of the *col legno* effect, changing higher and lower as the bow stick taps closer to and farther from the bridge. See *legno*. (Techniques No.2), *battuto*.

sul ponticello (It.) See *ponticello*.

suoni flautati (It.) See *flautando*.

tallone (talone) (It.) See *frog*.
> *al* __ At the frog.
> *col* __ At the frog.
> *sul* __ At the frog.

talón (F.) See *frog*.
> *au* __ At the frog.
> avec le __ At the frog.
> du __ At the frog.

tasto, *tastiera* (It.), *diapasón* (Sp.), *touche* (Fr.), *Griffbrett* (G.) Fingerboard.
> *sul tasto, sulla tastiera* (It.) *sobre el diapasón* (Sp.) *sur la touche* (F.) *am Griffbrett* (G.) Refers to bow placement *over the fingerboard* to obtain a soft, distant light tone quality on a string instrument. This should **not** be confused with *flautando*, although *flautando* is often played near or over the fingerboard.

tip, *head, point* (E.) *pointe* (F.), *punta, punto* (It.), *Spitze* (G.) The pointed end of the bow. Also refers to playing at the extreme upper part of the bow near the tip.

The Bow Head and its Component Parts

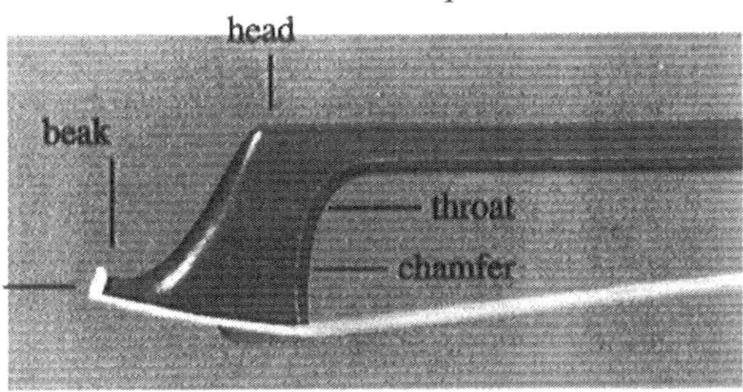

tire (F.) See *down-bow*.

tirer (F.) To draw a *down-bow*.
__ *avec le bois.*(F.) Draw with the wood of the bow. See *legno*
(Techniques No. 1), *bois, tratto*.

tone color (E.) Refers to the tonal quality of musical pitches and the
many available ways a composer may change the tonal characteristics
for expressive purpose. Twentieth century composers often request
gradual or sudden changes of tone color, much more often and with
more variety and scope than composers in the past. The Viennese composers, in particular Schönberg, Berg and Webern, developed *tone color*
as an integral structural expressive element in their music rivaling pitch,
rhythm and dynamics as musical material — an element they called
"Klangfarbenmelodie." Bow placement affects string *tone color* the
most. The three basic string tone colors are *normal* — bowing between
the bridge and the fingerboard, *sul tasto* — bowing over the fingerboard, and *sul ponticello* — bowing at or near the bridge. See *ordinario,
tasto, ponticello, Klangfarbenmelodie*.

Tonspinnen (G.) See *son filé*.

touche (F.) Fingerboard.
sur la __ On the fingerboard.
vers la __ Near the fingerboard. See *tasto*.

trainer (F.) To sustain or draw out a sound. "The opposite of *staccato*." (Brossard, *Dictionnaire de musique*, 1703).

tratto (It.) Drawn or bowed.

col legno __ drawn or bowed with the wood (stick). See *legno* (Techniques No.1).

tremolo (It.) The *tremolo* in modern usage characteristically consists of very small, unaccentuated *détaché* bow-strokes, usually performed near the bow-tip, though it may be nearer the middle when loud. In extreme forte, it may even be played at the frog of the bow. When a pitch is reiterated as many times as possible during the extent of its duration, with no specific time value placed on each stroke, the *tremolo* is said to be unmeasured. A *tremolo* may also be measured:

measured tremolo (E.), *non-tremolo, trémolo très régulier* (F.) *tremolo misurato* (It.). Does not employ the style of an unmeasured *tremolo*, but reiterates the exact number of bow-strokes notated. At times, confusion may result from the inexplicit nature of the notation of *tremolos*. Without specific indication, in some musical contexts, the musical example below could mean either to reiterate the notated pitch eight times in the rhythm of thirty-second notes or to reiterate the pitch as many times as possible within the duration of a quarter-note.

tremolo détaché (F.) *unmeasured tremolo* (E.) *tremolo rápido* (It., Sp.) *schnelles Tremolo* (G.) *trémolo serré* (literally "pressed") (F.) A rapid, unmeasured *tremolo*, usually as fast as possible. *Tremolo* is used extensively in twentieth century music in combination with other *tone color* techniques such as *sul ponticello, glissando, harmonics, sul tasto, noise* and *behind the bridge*.

Historically: (optional spellings: *tremulo, tremola, tremulus*).

1) Repeated notes in one bow stroke, not separated but marked by gentle pressure from the bow. This appears to have been measured whenever it was used. It is sometimes marked to be used on long notes (Marini, *Affetti musicali*, 1614) where its meaning is not completely clear (*tremolo con l'arco*), but it is usually marked with slurs or a wavy line over the repeated notes, which

are usually eighth notes.

Schütz, *Symphoniae Sacrae*, Part II, No. 27, 1647

Ex. 1

Couperin, *L'apothéose de Lulli*, 1724

Ex. 2

LeClair, *Troisième livre de sonatas*, 1734.

Ex. 3

Early examples of *tremolo*

The Schütz example above is a rare case in which the pitch of the notes grouped in one bow does not remain the same throughout; in virtually every other example of this type of *tremolo*, it is used on repeated notes only. Dictionary definitions of the *tremolo* in the seventeenth and early eighteenth centuries always describe it as imitating the organ *tremulant*: "According to the usage which one finds very often ... [the term is used] to instruct all those who play stringed instruments to make several notes on the same degree with a single bow stroke, as for imitating the tremblant of the organ." (Brossard, *Dictionnaire de musique*, 1703). It is mentioned by both North and Simpson (who does not approve of it) in England (North, "As to Musick", c. 1695, in Wilson (ed.), *Roger North on Music*, 1959; Simpson, *The Division Viol*, 1695). It is regarded by North as similar to what he calls the *tempered stoccata*. See *stoccato, tempered*.

2) Measured repeated notes with separate bows, an effect whose invention is claimed by Monteverdi (Il *combattimento di Tancredi e Clorinda* [1624]), though actually used earlier by Marini and others.

3) Unmeasured rapidly repeated notes with separate bows (the modern meaning); probably first used in this sense by Farina (*Capriccio stravagante*, 1627).

4) *Tremolo* is the term used for left-hand *vibrato* by Geminiani, Leopold Mozart and others. (Geminiani, *The Art of Playing on the Violin*, 1751; Mozart, *Versuch einer gründlichen Violinschule*, 1756).

underneath the strings (E.) See *bowing underneath the strings*.

up-bow (E.) When the bow-hand moves toward the instrument while bowing: symbol = V

vertical bowing (E.) A term which refers to a sighing, scraping sound made by sliding the bow along the length of the string instead of the usual perpendicular direction. The actual term, vertical, applies more to the cello and bass which are played vertically. Vertical bowing applied to the violin and viola is actually in a horizontal plane but toward the scroll and back along the fingerboard.

Viotti-bowing (E.) A bowing employed in some of the works of G. B. Viotti and made famous by him. The bowing consists of a series of two *slurred staccato* bow-strokes. The first of the two slurred articulations occurs on a rhythmically weaker portion of the beat, the second on a stronger portion of the beat. The first of the two slurred notes receives very little bow and is unaccentuated, and the second receives far more bow and is accentuated. [Accent marks are often employed in place of the *f* marks in the example below, although sometimes neither are used].

Kreutzer, 42 Studies, no. 36

Ex. 1

Ex. 2

Examples of *Viotti-bowing*

volante (It.) See *staccato, flying* (No. 5).

whipped bowing (E.) See *fouetté*.

whole bow gliding (E.) A style of bowing occasionally requested by twentieth century composers in which the bow is drawn its full length *frog* to *tip* — on every note (or small group of notes). *Whole bow gliding* can be performed either softly, with an airy tone, or quite loudly, with a rough, energetic, vigorous tone. There is no standard term for this bowing style. Composers will indicate that the passage in question should be played with whole bows, or instructions will be given such as "Use a whole bow on every note" or "Glide with the entire length of the bow."

PETITE DICTIONARY OF PIZZICATO
BY KENNETH SARCH
PIZZICATO

(It.) The art of plucking the strings of a musical instrument with the fingers. The first appearance of *pizzicato* is thought to be in Monteverdi's opera "Il Combattimento di Tancredi e Clorinda" in 1607. Until the close of the 19th century, pizzicato meant mostly to pluck the string with the index finger of the right hand. The expansion and variety of *pizzicato* techniques called for by 20th century composers has become so extensive that an entire section of *pizzicato* terms and techniques is presented here just on this one area of string playing.

DEFINITIONS

alternating fingers (E.) The alternate plucking with the first and second fingers: 1-2-1-2-1-2. This technique may be used for fast repetitions of the same note, fast pizzicato passages in general, or notes which alternate between two strings. Bracing the thumb on the side of the fingerboard can help stabilize the hand when alternating the fingers. Using the fingers in sequence to pluck the string may be used for certain rhythms which would be difficult to pluck with the same finger. As an example, plucking 4-3-2-1 for this rhythm is quite simple:

A five-finger school of pizzicato existed in the past in Italy; a technique using the thumb and four fingers of the right hand.

alternating left and right hands (E.) Alternating the *pizzicato* between the right and left hands is effective for fast or difficult passages. Various combinations of right and left hand patterns can be devised as well. A common use is to begin a *pizzicato* passage immediately following an arco passage with a left hand *pizzicato* to provide time for the player to palm the bow and prepare the right hand to continue plucking the string.

apoyando (Sp.) To rest upon; support - a technique taken from the guitar in which the right hand finger, after plucking the string, comes to rest on the adjacent string. The sound resulting from this technique is full, controlled, and deliberate.

arpeggiated pizzicato chords (E.) A *pizzicato* chord may be arpeggiated with the fingers or the thumb of the right hand. The speed of arpeggiation must be planned as well as the direction -- bottom to top or top to bottom -- often indicated with a wavy line for arpeggiation and an arrow for the direction:

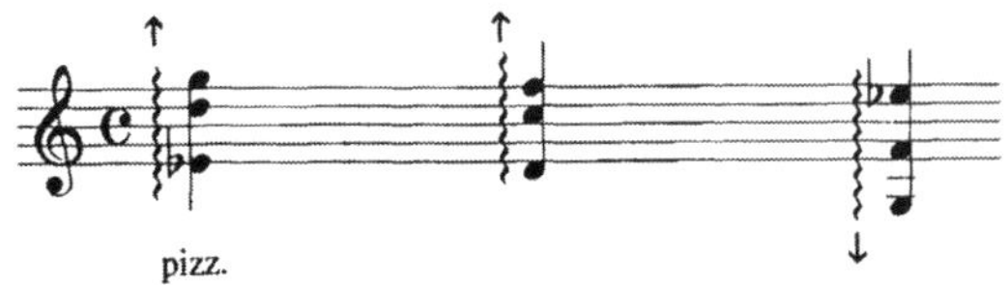

Example of *arpeggiated pizzicato chords*

banjo pizzicato (E.) See *pizzicato tremolo.*

Bartók pizzicato (E.) See *snap pizzicato.*

bisbigliando (It.) A term taken from the harp: plucking one string with the four fingers of the right hand in rapidly alternating sequence. See *alternating fingers.*

bi-tones (E.) Occur when both segments of a string on each side of a stopped note are vibrated, thus producing two distinct simultaneous tones from the same string. Often a by-product of left hand playing alone, *bi-tones* can be produced by a two-finger *pizzicato*, one finger plucking the string on one side, another finger plucking the string on the other side of the left hand finger stopping that string. *Bi-tones* can also be produced by a hard left hand slap or tap of the string. Bowing one side of the stopped note and plucking the other with the left hand will produce another type of *bi-tone* from the same string.

brush pizzicato (E.) See *guitar pizzicato.*

buzz pizzicato (E.) The string is plucked in the normal way and then allowed to vibrate against the fingernail of the finger which had just plucked the string thus creating a "buzz".

damping (E.) There are basically three ways to dampen a string after plucking it to immediately stop it from sounding:
1) clamping the string with the fingers of the left hand.
2) lifting the left hand fingers off the fingerboard but leaving them on the surface of the string thus effectively stopping it from vibrating. This produces an abrupt stop, like a *staccato.*
3) placing the right hand fingers upon the vibrating string or strings.

effleuré pizzicato (F.) From effleurer, 'to touch lightly'. The left hand fingers are placed lightly on the surface of the string (like playing a harmonic) so that a thump noise is created when the string is plucked instead of an actual pitch.

finger slap (E.) See *slap pizzicato.*

flicking (E.) A short, crisp *pizzicato* tone can be obtained by flicking the string with the second (long) finger of the right hand. To perform this, the bow is either palmed or put down. The nail of the second finger is placed against the lower part of the thumb forming a circle. The second finger is aimed at the appropriate string and then pushed against the thumb (toward the string). The thumb is opened releasing the second finger and allowing it to swing forward (straighten-

Right hand set to *flick* the string.

ing) to hit the string with the nail (like flicking a bug off the table). The speed of the fingernail hitting the string produces a "ping" as part of the *pizzicato* sound.

guitar pizzicato (E.) Plucking or strumming the string(s) with the thumb or brushing the strings with a sweep of the fingers.

guitar position (E.) The violin or viola is held in the lap or under the arm like a guitar and plucked with the thumb. One cannot deny the visual (theatrical) effect of the violin or viola held like a guitar, but some *pizzicato* passages are easier to negotiate in this manner. Although the cello could conceivably be held on the lap, its size and, of course, that of the double bass, makes guitar position awkward and ludicrous for these larger instruments. However, the violin and viola could be held **vertically** on the lap and plucked like a cello.

Example of *guitar position.*

left hand pizzicato (E.) Plucking the strings with the fingers of the left hand developed from guitar technique. Any lower finger (1, 2, or 3) or the open string may be plucked by any finger above it. When the 4th finger stops the string, that note must either be tapped with the tip of the bow to imitate a *pizzicato* sound, or plucked with the right hand. The usual markings for left hand *pizzicato* are the abbreviation *l.h. pizz.* or a + over the notehead. A dot is used to indicate which notes are to be hit with the bow.

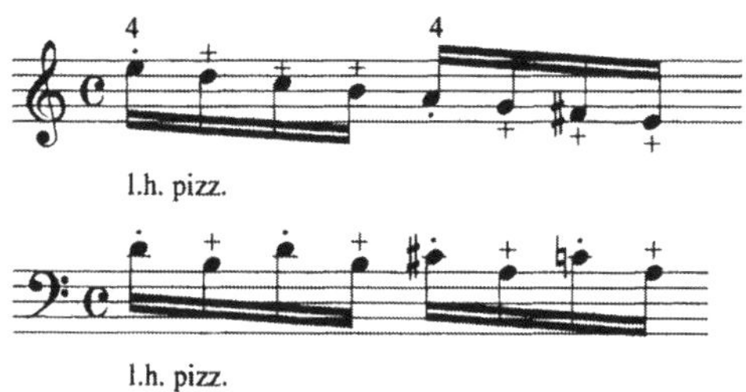

Examples of *left hand pizzicato*

Mitschlag (G.) A device used and named by Stefan Wolpe which consists of simultaneously plucking with the left hand (or with the index finger of the right hand at the frog) the note that is bowed and sustained. See *simultaneous arco* and *pizzicato*.

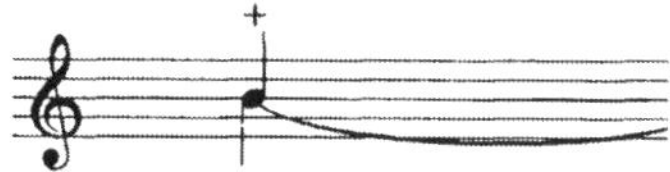

Example of the notation for *Mitschlag*

nail pizzicato (E.) The string is plucked with the edge of the fingernail of the right hand producing a hard, biting, metallic tone. See *buzz pizzicato*.

palm the bow (E.) To maneuver the bow into the palm of the bow hand so that the thumb is free to brace the hand (usually on the side of the fingerboard) and the index finger free to pluck the string.

pegbox pizzicato (E.) To pluck the strings in the pegbox (between the nut and the pegs). The sound produced is somewhat soft and limited to a type of short ping. Therefore it is rarely used and remains an effect. An example is found in Theodore Antoniou's *Four Likes for Solo Violin*.

pinch pizzicato (E.) Plucking the string by grasping it with the thumb and another finger, pulling the string while squeezing it until it slips back and vibrates.

pizzicato (It.) The art of plucking the strings of a musical instrument with the fingers. The first appearance of *pizzicato* is thought to be in

Monteverdi's opera "Il Combattimento di Tancredi e Clorinda" in 1607. Until the close of the 19th century, *pizzicato* meant mostly to pluck the string with the index finger of the right hand.

pizzicato glissando (It.) After the string has been plucked, a glissando can be effected by sliding the finger stopping the string either up or down. The finger must be pressed rather firmly on the string for the glissando to sound. If the string is stopped with the edge of the nail of the left hand finger stopping the string, a louder, longer lasting glissando results.

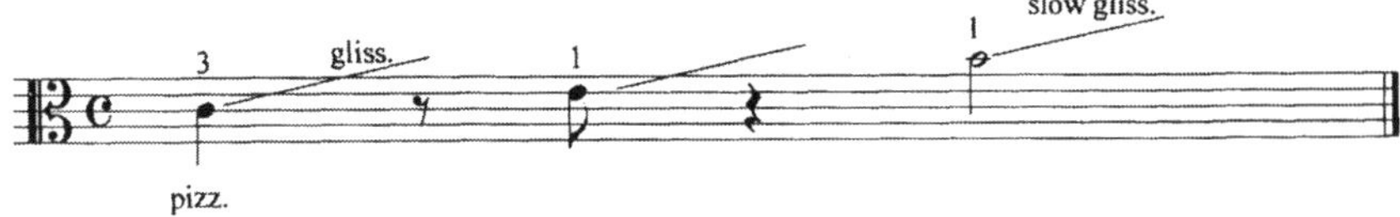

Example of *pizzicato glissando*

pizzicato harmonics (E.) The string player performs *pizzicato harmonics* in the same way as it is done on the guitar or harp: To produce clear *pizzicato harmonics*, the finger of the left hand lightly touches a node exactly as for a bowed harmonic. The string is then plucked and the finger touching the node is quickly lifted to allow the plucked harmonic to ring. The finger is replaced on a node to prepare for the next *pizzicato harmonic.*

Example of *pizzicato harmonics*

pizzicato location (E.) Where the string is plucked along the string determines both the quality of sound and the volume:

middle (over the fingerboard) plucking the string at the midpoint (measured from the nut or the finger stopping the string to the bridge) produces the fullest, roundest, warmest tone in pizzicato. The middle of the string offers the greatest amplitude of the vibrating string.

¾ distance (near the end of the fingerboard) produces nearly as much volume, but the tone quality is more brittle, brighter and not as mellow as in the middle.

between fingerboard and bridge (normal bow area) produces a harsh, aggressive twang, quite accented and strong.

at the bridge (*ponticello*) produces a nasal, brittle attack with soft volume. The nail can be used at the bridge to pluck the string for a clearer sound.

behind the bridge produces a soft, high *pizzicato* with a rather tense quality. Only one high indeterminate pitch can be obtained on each string behind the bridge.

in the pegbox (between the nut and the pegs) See *pegbox pizzicato.*

pizzicato muta (Sp.) Adopted from the guitar, the string is plucked with the thumb while the lower part of the palm dampens the string. This technique works better on the cello and the bass.

pizzicato tremolo (*tremolando*) (It.) A rapid repetition of a note or notes played on a string instrument pizzicato by a back and forth strumming of the right hand index finger or thumb. The notation will have *tremolo* lines on the note stem, will indicate *pizzicato tremolo*, or be written out in quick note values usually with arrows or ⊓ and v to show the direction of the alternations.

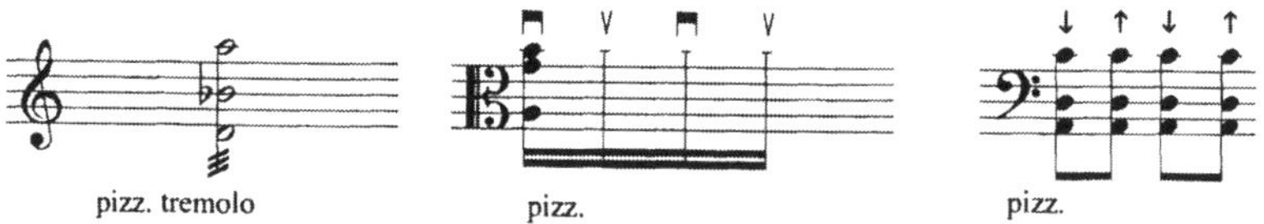

Example of *pizzicato tremolo*

pizzicato vibrato (It.) Designates that the note or passage to be played *pizzicato* must also be played with vibrato. If this indication is not present, the performer may choose to play the *pizzicato* notes without vibrato, or at least, with very little vibrato.

plectrum pizzicato (E.) The strings are plucked with a guitar, banjo or mandolin pick.

pluck (E.) To pull on and quickly release the string or strings of a musical instrument with the finger or fingers so that the string vibrates to produce a musical tone called *pizzicato.*

ponticello pizzicato (It.) Plucking the string at the bridge. See *pizzicato location.*

reverse pizzicato (E.) Plucking or strumming the four strings in the opposite direction from normal - for violin and viola, *reverse pizzicato* means from the high string toward the low (normal is from low to high); for cello and bass, *reverse pizzicato* means from the low string toward the high string. The reason for this difference is that for violin and viola, the high string is closest to the bow arm; whereas for cello and bass, the low string is closest to the bow arm.

scooping (E.) Using the first (index) or second (long) finger, the string player places the lower side of the finger tip under the string and plucks it by pronating the arm (turning clockwise) and lifting upwards in a scooping motion. *Scooping* produces a mellow, resonant *pizzicato* with a gentle attack. *Scooping* can also be done with the thumb by placing it under the string and scooping upwards in a similar manner.

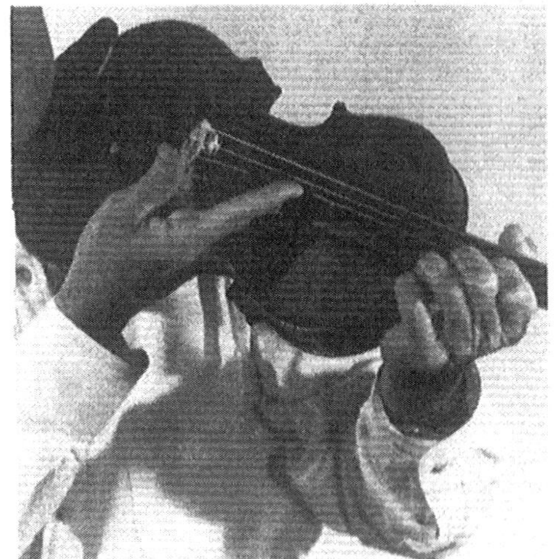

The right hand set to *scoop* the string.

simultaneous arco and pizzicato (E.) The string player may bow on one string while simultaneously plucking another string with the left hand. Open string *pizzicato* is often used because it is loud, but stopped notes can also be plucked while bowing. A well know example of this technique is found in the third movement violin cadenza and at the end of the second movement of the Bartók *Contrasts.* It is also possible to pluck the note on the same string which the player is bowing, beginning an *arco* note with a *pizzicato* attack. See *Mitschlag.*

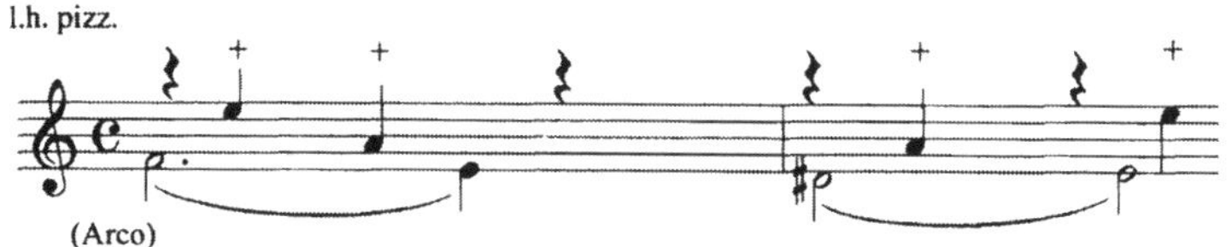

Example of *simultaneous arco* and *pizzicato*

slap pizzicato (E.) (finger slap) Developed as a jazz technique on the double bass, the player strikes the strings, usually over the fingerboard, with the open (right) hand (like a slap) producing a percussive 'clack' against the fingerboard.

slurred pizzicato (E.) Two or more notes fingered quickly after a single pluck of the string creating the impression of *legato*. *Slurred pizzicato* must be played so that each *legato* group after the string is plucked remains on the same string.

Examples of *slurred pizzicato*

snap pizzicato (E.) A loud, percussive effect performed on a string instrument by holding the string between two fingers (usually thumb and long finger), lifting the string upwards and releasing it so that it snaps back to hit the fingerboard with a strong 'bang' or 'snap'. In addition to the percussive slap, the pitch is also heard. This technique is sometimes called the *Bartók Pizzicato* because Bartók popularized its usage in his string quartets and other string writing. It is often indicated by the sign:

Example of *snap* or *Bartók pizzicato*

strum (E.) Sweeping or brushing the fingers or thumb across the strings producing a chord, usually in a rhythmic and controlled manner.

tapping (E.) Another left hand technique taken from the guitar. The finger is dropped with speed upon the string producing a thump on the fingerboard along with a soft *pizzicato* type tone. *Tapping* creates an unusual effect when used in orchestral or chamber music works where the quantity of players makes up for the individual small volume. String players are familiar with *tapping* the string as a way of softly testing a finger placement for pitch.

thumb pizzicato (E.) Plucking the strings with the thumb produces full, clear *pizzicato* tones in a wide dynamic range. On the cello and bass, *thumb pizzicato* is performed in the opposite direction to finger *pizzicato* (from low string to high string), that is, the thumb is shoved across the strings pushing or lifting instead of pulling the string as in *pizzicato* with the fingers.

two finger pizzicato (E.) Holding onto a string with two fingers (index and long) and plucking that string with both fingers at once makes a loud, strong *pizzicato* with a forceful accent. This technique works best for single *pizzicato* notes to be played loudly and aggressively. Double stops can be plucked with *two finger pizzicato* (triple and quadruple stops with three and four fingers) by holding each string with a different finger and plucking all the strings involved simultaneously.

two hand pizzicato (E.) Plucking the strings with the left and right hands simultaneously or in alternation. In this way, it is possible to play two simple *pizzicato* lines in counterpoint, to alternate one hand with the other, or to play two different strings, open or stopped, at the same time or in quick succession. See *alternating left and right hands*.

finis

AUTHOR BIOGRAPHIES

Barbara Garvey Jackson has degrees from the University of Illinois, The Eastman School of Music and Stanford (Ph.D.). She studied modern violin with Paul Rolland, Andre de Rebaupierre and Sandor Salgo; historic violin with Marilyn MacDonald; and musicology with Putnam Adlric. Dr. Jackson is Professor Emerita of Music at the University of Arkansas and is editor and publisher of ClarNan Editions, a desk-top publishing company which specializes in historic music composed by women.

Joel Berman has degrees from Juilliard, Columbia University and the University of Michigan (D.M.A.). His teachers have included Edouard Dethier, Robert Mann and D.C. Dounis. He has been a faculty member at the University of Maryland during which time he served as conductor of the Jewish Community Center Orchestra (Rockville, MD). Dr. Berman has appeared as violin soloist and chamber music musician throughout the United States and abroad. He is currently concertmaster and soloist with the American Camerata for New Music and is currently performing chamber music concerts, lecturing and recording.

Kenneth Sarch, with degrees from Juilliard, New England Conservatory and Boston University (D.M.A.), has studied with Ivan Galamian, Dorothy DeLay, Sally Thomas, Robert Koff and Roman Totenberg. He has taught at Boston University, New England Conservatory, Shenandoah Conservatory, Hartford Conservatory, East Tennessee State University and as a Fulbright scholar in Brazil. Recitals and USIA Arts America grants have taken him to Europe, Canada, Central and South America and the Middle East. Author of The Twentieth Century Violin, Dr. Sarch is currently on the faculty at Mansfield University and serves also as concertmaster of the Williamsport Symphony in Pennsylvania.